AMERICAN MISFIT: IN SEARCH OF REALITY

AMERICAN MISFIT: IN SEARCH OF REALITY

MATTHEW MOTYKA

COMMON GROUND

First published in 2025
as part of New Directions in the Humanities Book Imprint
Common Ground Research Networks

University of Illinois Research Park
2001 South First St, Suite 201 L
Champaign, IL 61820 USA

Library of Congress Cataloging-in-Publication Data

Names: Motyka, Matthew J., author.
Title: American misfit : in search of reality / by Matthew Motyka.
Description: Champaign, IL : Common Ground Research Networks, 2025. |
  Summary: "The intellectual justification of American Misfit is Paul
  Ricoeur's theory of narrative, which explores the role and significance
  of narrative in human understanding and interpretation of the world. He
  emphasizes the hermeneutic dimension of narratives, suggesting that they
  are a means by which we interpret our existence. In his quest, Matthew
  Motyka tries to make sense of his multicultural experiences, which
  happened to him quite unexpectedly. He grew up in communist Poland,
  spent his twenties in France, and finally moved to the United States. As
  he becomes a successful immigrant and appreciates what America has to
  offer a newcomer, he asks a troubling question: Why does America,
  despite its apparent generosity to outsiders, not give itself over to
  being fully loved? In search of an answer, he turns to the ideas and
  experiences of European intellectuals who have reflected on issues of
  uprootedness, immigration, and alienation"-- Provided by publisher.
Identifiers: LCCN 2024057947 (print) | LCCN 2024057948 (ebook) | ISBN
  9781966214090 (hardback) | ISBN 9781966214106 (paperback) | ISBN
  9781966214113 (adobe pdf)
Subjects: LCSH: Motyka, Matthew J. | Immigrants--United States--Biography.
  | Europe--Intellectual life.
Classification: LCC CT275.M65376 A3 2025 (print) | LCC CT275.M65376
  (ebook) | DDC 973.9092 [B]--dc23/eng/20250111
LC record available at https://lccn.loc.gov/2024057947
LC ebook record available at https://lccn.loc.gov/2024057948

ISBN: 978-1-966214-09-0 (HBK)
ISBN: 978-1-966214-10-6 (PBK)
ISBN: 978-1-966214-11-3 (pdf)

DOI: 10.18848/ 978-1-966214-11-3/CGP

Cover Design: Phillip Kalantzis Cope
Cover Image: Shutterstock (2123458328)

TABLE OF CONTENTS

ACKNOWLEDGEMENTS

I would like to express my deepest gratitude to all those who took the time to read this manuscript and provide valuable feedback. Their careful attention, insightful suggestions, and thoughtful critiques have greatly enriched this work.

Special thanks to Cathal Doherty, SJ, for his meticulous editing and for helping to refine the clarity and flow of the manuscript. Thanks to Melinda Ericson and Antoni Uçerler, SJ, for their encouragement and advice in seeing this work through to completion.

I am also grateful to Lissa McCullough for her insights into the work of Simone Weil and Leszek Kołakowski, and to Anna Kidacka for referring me to Tzvetan Todorov's book *L'homme dépaysé*.

Finally, I would like to thank the University of San Francisco for granting me a sabbatical that allowed me to spend a year at Loyola Marymount University (LMU), where most of the writing took place. I am truly grateful for the generosity of LMU's Jesuit community and its rector, Eddie Siebert, SJ, for creating the conditions in which I could fully immerse myself in the project.

Introduction: A Word About the Method

The methodology I have adopted for *American Misfit: In Search of Reality* is a hybrid approach that combines personal experience on a backdrop of historical events that have shaped that experience for the past half a century. One of the intellectual warrants for this method is Paul Ricoeur's narrative theory that, in my view, valorizes such an approach to writing.[1] A personal story represents a thread within the fabric of historical contingencies that make up a generalized view of history. Drafting and juxtaposing personal stories illustrate the impact of historical events on shaping one's individual consciousness and, ultimately, one's identity.

Ricoeur's narrative theory explores the role and significance of narratives in human understanding and interpretation of the world. He argues that narratives are fundamental to our experience of time, identity, and meaning. He emphasizes the hermeneutic dimension of narratives, suggesting that they are a means through which we make sense of our existence. This was precisely my motivation to write a book that would help me to make sense of my own circumstances as a successful immigrant to the country of wide-ranging possibilities for personal growth and fulfillment. This motivation often took the shape of an obsessive quest for justification and affirmation of my current position in the society with

---

[1] I base my explanation of Ricoeur's narrative theory on the following sources: Paul Ricoeur, *Temps et Récit* [Time and Narrative] (Paris: Editions du Seuil, 1983); Paul Ricoeur, "Mimesis and Representation," in *A Ricoeur Reader: Reflection and Imagination*, ed. Mario J. Valdés (Toronto: Toronto University Press, 1991), 137–155; Paul Ricoeur, "Narrated Time," in *A Ricoeur Reader: Reflection and Imagination*, ed. Mario J. Valdés (Toronto: Toronto University Press, 1991), 338–154; Paul Ricoeur, "Time Traversed: Remembrance of Things Past," in *A Ricoeur Reader: Reflection and Imagination*, ed. Mario J. Valdés (Toronto: Toronto University Press, 1991), 355–189; Paul Ricoeur, "Narrative Identity," trans. David Wood, in *On Paul Ricoeur: Narrative and Interpretation*, ed. David Wood, Warwick Studies in Philosophy and Literature (London: Routledge, 1991), 188–99; Paul Ricoeur. *From Text to Action: Essays in Hermeneutics*, II, trans. Kathleen Blamey & John B. Thomson (Evanston: Northwestern University Press, 1991); Paul Ricoeur. *Philosophie, éthique et politique: Entretiens et dialogues* [Philosophie, Ethics, and Politics: Interviews and Dialogues], ed. Catherine Goldenstein (Paris: Editions du Seuil, 2017).

which I could not share much affect except for a feeling of dutiful gratitude. By seeking self-understanding, I wanted to explain first to myself and then to readers the influence of the context in which I happened to live.

To explain how narratives function, Ricoeur introduces the concept of "threefold mimesis." The first level is prefiguration, where the narrative anticipates future events and establishes expectations. This process could be envisioned as gestation of the ideas before they become intelligible to me as the author and then to the potential reader. The realization of this intelligibility happens at the second level that Ricoeur names "configuration," where the events of the narrative unfold and acquire meaning. He further explores the temporal dimension of narratives, highlighting the interplay between emplotment and explanation. Emplotment involves organizing events into a coherent narrative structure, while explanation involves understanding the causal relations between events. Ricoeur argues that narratives provide a framework for comprehending the complex temporal nature of human existence. In my own writing process, the work involved first remembrance and then the ordering of the events into the autobiographical sequence. Remembrance and ordering of autobiographical events were a complex process involving occasionally painful review of past events that had emotionally formative (or deformative) impacts on my development as a person.

Ricoeur's third level is "refiguration," where the narrative resonates with the reader's own experiences and prompts reflection and interpretation. As a writer, I have had in mind imaginary readers with whom I would share my own experience hoping that we will find echoes of the same quest for affirming our identities. In fact, this process of preserving or reconstructing identity is at the heart of Ricoeur's preoccupations with how narratives contribute to the formation of personal and collective identities. He suggests that our identities are not fixed but, rather, evolving and shaped by the stories we tell about ourselves and others. Through narrative, we create a sense of continuity and coherence in our lives.

Through the reflective process, I sought the authority of thinkers I admire to help me shape my ideological outlook on the world. These encounters have resulted in affirming my difference; my own particular story has been validated by the ideas found in the writings of the intellectuals whose erudition and analytical acumen provided me with tools rehabilitating my identity. Their works have contributed to preserving and valorizing the connection to my ethnic roots despite pressures from American culture to sever that continuity and give in to the generalized uprootedness of my host country's culture.

According to Ricoeur, narratives have ethical implications. He emphasizes the role of narratives in fostering empathy, understanding, and solidarity among individuals and communities. He suggests that engaging with diverse narratives can expand our moral horizons and contribute to a more inclusive and just society. By presenting my own story on the backdrop of history, I first deal with my own conflicting impulses toward the reality in which history constrained me to live. By having recourse to external insights of thinkers such as Simone Weil, Leszek Kołakowski, Tzvetan Todorov, and Alain Finkielkraut, I seek ethical resolutions to my initial impulse of rejection toward the cultural alterity of my host county. Reading and discussing philosophical insights of these intellectuals have provided me with the sense of empathy toward the culture that has constructed itself on its own uprootedness. By reading and writing about my own struggles to fit in, I have undergone the process of reaching the attitude of compassion and solidarity with that otherness. By the same token, my hope as an author is that I might reach a readership that would respond to my own story with empathy and understanding of my predicament as an alien resident who tries to preserve his identity made fragile by the surroundings that want one to assimilate to their own uprootedness. By providing this autobiographical material, I offer my own experience for the benefit of those who might try to understand why people act in certain ways. For those who seek an understanding of their own predicament in the life story of others, my account, which is necessarily an interpretation, represents substance for the subsequent level of interpretation. By striving to preserve my identity through the ordering of my own life experience, I offer autobiographical matter that might be a source of empathy for those who read it.

Where I depart from Ricoeur's analysis is the fact that my story is not fiction. Ricoeur's work on narratives centers essentially on works of literary fiction or historical narratives. In that sense, there might be some discrepancy between my claim to write a sort of confession that relates lived experience and Ricoeur's focus on fiction writing that incorporates elements of real life. My writing is essentially based on memory and intends to bring coherence and self-understanding of this autobiographical story. The events that punctate its flow are real and connect. Whereas a work of fiction intends to imitate life (mimesis in Aristotle's notion referred to by Ricoeur), autobiographical writing does not imitate life in the sense of creating a fictional world by borrowing from life. It does not invent the events that the author lived, but the author's creative process lies essentially in providing coherence to the events that might not have in appearance any inner logic. Where a fiction storyteller meets an autobiographical narrator is the process of selecting events that help explanation and interpretation of the past events. In both cases, we have the process of emplotment that forces the flow of events into a manageable timeframe surrendered to the exigencies of the purpose both storytellers have devised. The historical and objective notion of time surrenders in the process of emplotment to a subjective intentionality of the author. The subjectivized time leads the autobiographical narrative to an end that is essentially ethical. As mentioned before, it intends to do both: seek and show empathy, and create a sense of solidarity between the writer and the reader. Ricoeur states in *Time and Narrative*, "We tell stories because in the last analysis human lives need and merit being narrated" (p. 75). By unveiling a personal story of successful transfer to the United States, I intend for my autobiographical narrative to help readers build empathy. Yet it also shows the price of that successful transplant mainly through suggesting the necessary alienation to the world that has in actuality very little in common with my past context. The story begs for empathy by staging episodes that are not to be found in America. At the same time, my story offers a view of America that, through its originality, might be perceived as a love letter to the lover who cannot understand the meandering of a life, a letter that expresses gratitude and empathy for America that has all it takes to be closer to one's heart but cannot achieve it. It is a story of uprootedness yet also a forceful attachment to one's roots. Uprootedness is a very significant concept, charged with meaning that Simone Weil uses to explain the ills of modern society. Kołakowski and Todorov know the dilemma of uprootedness from their own experience of immigrants in Europe and from their periodic work at American universities. These philosophers show how cultural neoliberalism has not only liberated societies from their attachment to tradition but also weakened their sense of belonging.

My book relates a life that begins in the complex fabric of the second half of the 20th century and continues in the first half of the subsequent century. It aims to communicate the struggle one must undertake to protect one's identity in face of an overpowering impact of the culture that, despite its generosity, naturally imposes its imprint on newcomers. I try to explain the reasons for resistance my inner self foments despite a deep respect springing from my own ethnic background that cherishes anything that comes from America as a carrier of progressive values. My expectation is that readers will appreciate my approach which involves research first in one's own past marked affectively by historical events and insights from thinkers whose ideas have influenced my own worldview of an immigrant in quest of his own place in the limitless landscape of simmering possibilities beckoning to newcomers with an invitation to lose their soul. From an ethical point of view, my story also holds potential for readers to explore personal and social transformation of their own.

Prologue

> A cybernaut ... abandons the obscene materiality of things for the endless
> delights of an insubstantial space. He was geographical and historical, here he
> is angelic, withdrawn like the angels from the fatigue of life on earth and the
> order of incarnation, equipped like them with the gift of ubiquity and that of
> weightlessness.... he is delivered from the past ... and from that presence in oneself
> of the dead that we call ... identity.
> (Alain Finkielkraut, *L'Humanité perdue* [Lost Humanity] [152, my translation])

Echoing Alain Finkielkraut's words, this book has the modest ambition of taking
readers on an introspective journey into the recent European past that preceded
the proliferation of digital media. It attempts to draw a canvas of events that still
possessed the sense of a spatiotemporal distance. The conquest of that space
required time and the kind of intellectual and physical effort that digital reality
has nearly obliterated. That conquest implied above all a conquest of the self
in a lengthy process of circumventing the otherness of the new territory. Today
cybernauts navigate digital space instantaneously, leaving aside the lengthy
requirement of inculturation through mastery of language and familiarity with
culture. Perhaps only refugees still need to learn how to fit into the host country's ways to establish a new permanent existence there. The book explores the
fear that most of the humanity has become consumers of alterity with respect
to tourism rather than eager partakers of what the Other has to propose, which
would certainly enrich those who show a degree of openness to it. The book
depicts sequences of memories the author has recorded from his early life in
Europe and from frequent returns to the continent after he established himself
in the United States. It also offers insights about contemporary America from
a standpoint of a European "expat." In fact, this double distance from both
Europe and America makes it possible for the author to offer the perspective of

an outsider, not necessarily objective, but certainly detached from the national passions that blind the insider. The year of 2019 marked the 75th anniversary of D-Day and the 30th anniversary of the fall of the Iron Curtain. The horrors of the Nazi occupation of Europe and intellectual and economic oppression within the Eastern Bloc have become a distant memory about which the young generation learns from textbooks or documentaries. The book weaves a subjective narrative of life in a world arbitrarily divided by historical entanglements.

This first-person narrative constitutes a reflection that argues for the importance of cultural roots. My tale is in part inspired by Simone Weil's *The Need for Roots: Prelude to a Declaration of Duties Toward Mankind (1949)* [*L'Enracinement, prélude à une déclaration des devoirs envers l'être humain*]. Weil (1909–1943) was a French philosopher and political activist on behalf of the working class, as well as an engaged supporter of the French Resistance in London in World War II. In *The Need for Roots*, which was intended to be a draft of a vision for France after the liberation, Weil challenged the way history was being taught in schools. She sees the study of history as an essential component of one's sense of rootedness. Her statement about writing history as it was done in France seems to be almost commonplace in today's poststructuralist, postcolonial era: Conquerors impose their historical perspective on facts and interpret them to justify the political status quo that serves their interests. History as a discipline has become a casualty of the conquerors' political pressures and subjected to the supreme rule of force in the world. "No attention is paid to the defeated. [History] is a scene of a Darwinian process more pitiless still than that which governs animal and vegetable life" (212). Discussing questions about the historical method, Weil asks provocatively whether history should be taught at all, or selectively, for example, by placing wars in the background. To dismiss any doubt about her stance on the issue, she brings up the example of the United States, the country that, in her view, epitomizes a lack of a historical perspective ("We have only to look at the United States to see what it is to have a people deprived of the time-dimension," 221).

Weil associates the surrender of historiography to the political agenda of the governing body with the rise of the state as a political entity in the second half of the Renaissance and its subsequent evolution under the auspices of absolutist ideology. At the court of Versailles in the 17th century, absolutism reached its apogee in surrendering culture (including historical viewpoint) to the service of the absolutist monarchy. History as a handmaid of the political power became a vehicle of the ideology of conquest and served the propagandist apparatus of the body politic. Its ideological framework became a source of theories that attempted to focus on unstoppable social evolution and were used as ideological warrants for various political regimes. For Weil, Marxist theory is one of the fruits of this development of historiography. She argues, "Marxism is nothing else than a belief in a mechanism of this sort. There the force is given the name of history; it takes the form of the class struggle; justice is relegated to some future time which has to be preceded by a sort of apocalyptic cataclysm" (231). The Polish philosopher Leszek Kołakowski (1927–2009) was an expert on Marxism both in theory and from his personal experience of living within a system that claimed to be based on Marx's "scientific" theory. He wrote a monumental study called *Main Currents of Marxism* (1978). His views of Marxism echo Weil's mistrust. His critical positions toward the ideological framework of the Polish pro-Soviet government during a student rebellion in 1968 ultimately cost him his academic position at the University of Warsaw and led to exile in the West. In his acceptance speech for the first Kluge Prize from the Library of Congress in 2003, called "What the Past Is For," Kołakowski states:

> Human history is a collection of unpredictable accidents, and we can all easily cite any number of instances where an event that was clearly decisive in shaping the destiny of mankind for subsequent decades or centuries could have gone a different way than it did; there was nothing necessary in its happening or in its results.... Alas, all the predictions made by Marx or, later, by Marxists, were demonstrably false; social development went in an entirely different direction.

I accept the opinion that Marxism is probably right in its assumption that great masses of humanity have been economically and culturally uprooted; given its materialist scope, however, it ignores the fact that the dominating classes are uprooted as well, in a spiritual sense. As the ideological instrument of a governing class, Marxism uproots individuality from its historical context and drives its ideological engine to some imaginary future at the expense of spiritual fulfillment in the present. Weil's *The Need for Roots* deplores the loss of roots in her contemporary France. She writes, "To be rooted is perhaps the most important and least recognized need of the human soul" (41). "Whoever is uprooted himself uproots others. Whoever is rooted doesn't uproot others" (45). The current ills of our world thus spring from the condition of uprootedness. The cultures of the West are fruits of that deviation, which has led political development toward obfuscating and disconnecting from truth. The fruits of this deviation from truth have been deceitful ideologies basing their self-confidence on self-referential idols in order to camouflage the truth about the human condition—"Idolatry is an armour that prevents pain from entering the soul" (217).

How did this happen? When and how has the link between the origin and the purpose of the world been severed? In my personal multicultural scope, I will attempt to find, in the cultures I know, ideological justifications for the political reality they helped to enforce. Through the intimate journey of my experience, I will seek to understand the forces at work in those cultures and their logic in warranting their policies regarding the place of the individual in the body politic. Even though Simone Weil's lucid evaluation of the Western world's cultural position is highly idealistic, her perspective helps to purge the outgrowths of ideologies that have overshadowed the original connection of human beings with the true purpose of their existence: the pursuit of truth.

As a generalization, we can summarize Weil's view in the following sentence: Since the Renaissance the West has found itself on a wrong track paved by force and pride, and Hitler's assent to power has been a logical consequence of this trajectory. Weil wrote her *Need for Roots* in London in 1943 during the German occupation of France. How accurate she was in her critique of her times may be verified against the philosophical writings of a few intellectuals from the late 20th and 21st centuries, such as the already cited Leszek Kołakowski, Tzvetan Todorov, or Alain Finkielkraut, to whose work I will refer in the subsequent chapters.

For Weil, spirituality is the remedy for a world wrapped in a veil of lies with no awareness of it: "There is only one possible choice to be made. Either we must perceive at work in the universe, alongside force, a principle of a different kind, or else we must recognize force as being the unique and sovereign ruler over human relations also" (230). The spiritual sphere lies above the carnal sphere "where good is only good ... where evil is only evil ..." (192). To reach that realm requires an ascetic ascent of the mind; many philosophical and religious traditions have elaborated methods that help one go beyond the level of our confusing thoughts, oscillating between good and evil to reach the domain of perfect clarity from which the subject might undergo illumination leading to the heart of truth. Truth can be reached only through love: "Truth is a radiant manifestation of reality" (242).

What has Polish culture given to me that has produced the fruit that represents my selfhood? What was the import of French culture in pruning outgrowths of *polonitude* (a mixed feeling oscillating between an inferiority complex and a superiority complex)? What nourishments and what toxicity did the social political context dispense for my growth? How does Polish culture relate to other European cultures? How has my American experience changed my self-image and my view of these three cultures, which have had a formative impact on who I have become? These are some of the questions this book intends to touch upon. Given the autobiographical framework of this undertaking, I feel encouraged to quote Michel de Montaigne's address to the reader of his *Essays*, "... c'est moy que ie peins. Mes defauts s'y liront au vif et ma forme naifue, autant que la reuerence publique me l'a permis. [... it is myself I paint. My defects are therein to be read to the life, and any imperfections and my natural form, so far as public reverence hath permitted me]."[1] Even though I am the main subject of this project, I am not a center; instead, I am matter to be dissected in order to reveal the truth about the land, the people, and their forms of life.

---

[1] Michel de Montaigne, *Essays*, trans. Charles Cotton (Stanford University Press, 1962).

PART I

The Grain

CHAPTER 1

Krzyszkowice: The Grain of a Spiky Plant

The vast majority lived in a sense of normalcy only interrupted at times; people attended schools and universities, stood out for various positions in administration, got married and divorced, having no sense of alienation from the country where they lived, a non-sovereign country, whose governments they did not choose, based on an already laughable ideology which nobody took seriously.

(Leszek Kołakowski, "PRL—Wesoły nieboszczyk?" [Polish People's Republic—A Merry Corpse?] [My translation])

A summer day in a village near Kraków. The creek runs peacefully through the meadow, refreshed by newly grown grass after the first hay harvest, intended as winter forage for the cattle. The mown grass dries in the Sun to be compiled into haystacks, creating a unique Eastern European landscape, often reproduced by painters. It's already past St. John's Day, which is celebrated on June 24, and therefore bathing is permitted in the creek and it doesn't come with the risk of catching a rough Eastern European cold. Local boys gather by the creek and jump into its refreshing waters. There is no warning of the dramatic surprise that we the children of the village are about to experience. Tadek suddenly screams, "Look, look, guys, a bomb, over there, at the bottom of the creek. The only girl among us, Ela, shouts, 'Don't get any closer, don't get any closer, it might explode!' We need to tell Mrs. Motykowa so that she can call the fire station in the town." Mrs. Motykowa, my mother, is a teacher at the local grammar school, known in the neighborhood as a kind of matron gifted with an unusually pronounced common sense. Her advice is often solicited by villagers in diverse emergency situations, be it illness, an accident, a need for some written documents, or a phone call. There are three telephones in the village: at school, in the presbytery, and in our house, a sort of lifeline cleverly secured by my mother when the commune office relocated to a different place, allowing the teachers to move to the building. This former manor, that used to belong to a family of nobles exiled by the pro-Soviet communist government in Poland, is now a residence for the local public school's teachers, including my family. A couple of hours later, members of the Volunteer Fire Department come and look at the misfired bomb. It appears to be just an empty shell, its content having been washed away by waters of the creek. This was in around 1965. Only 20 years after the end of World War II.

For children of about 10 years old, 20 years seem an eternity. Looking back from the perspective of half a century, 20 years appears to be a surprisingly short time.

Only in the autumn of my life have I realized how much of my early upbringing was influenced by the ravages of that terrible war, from which the generation of my parents had never recovered. The horrors of the war were my parents' memories and, for me, a post–World War II child, these war stories were formative mythical tales, received with a feeling of pride in my parents' heroic survival and a sense of guilt for being born at the time when there was no longer a chance to be heroic.

My mother had been a teenager when Germany occupied Poland in 1939. She and her siblings had lost their mother just a few years before. My grandfather remarried a woman who disliked the children from his first marriage and discriminated against them even more once the war began. They were burdensome mouths to feed at a time of severe shortages of food. When my mother fell ill with appendicitis during the German occupation, with no recourse to medical care, she remained immobilized in a chair for several months. Her father fed her while the stepmother visited only to ask if she was still alive.

I think that miracle of surviving appendicitis without surgery made my mother that woman who was indeed not afraid of anything. After the war, she dreamed of becoming a doctor but could not afford to go to medical school and was not accepted to train as a nurse because of a heart condition. As a compromise, she ended up becoming an elementary school teacher and, ultimately, that Mrs. Motykowa who, in the eyes of the villagers, had solutions for every possible problem.

I am looking at a few pictures I took with me when leaving Poland in 1981. They show our family gatherings, my parents, my aunts and uncles, my cousins, our dog, and the "manor" with a grove in the background that someone called "schadzki" [trysts]. The name alluded to the romantic encounters of teachers, who were predominantly females, with their heart's interests or, perhaps, between villagers seeking seclusion for their clandestine love affairs. Of course, for me, in this prepubescent period, the name had a different connotation—I even pronounced the word as the villagers did in their local dialect, *sotzki*, without any awareness of the erotic connotations of the word. My main memories of schadzki are summer morning outings to the grove with my father, who showed me bushes of wild raspberries. The touch of fresh dew on leaves, the taste of ripe berries, and a rare instance of receiving my father's attention as he tried to teach me something about nature—all of these have fixed this cheerful image in my brain. It comes back even at the sight of a plastic Costco container of raspberries.

My father was a good storyteller. He was 25 years older than my mother and had been actively involved in the military reconstruction of Poland after World War I and in the battles after Hitler invaded in 1939. My cousins, of whom the majority were older than me, listened to his accounts of his adventures with acute attention. They grew prouder than me for having a relative who was decorated in his 20s with a *Virtuti Militari* medal by the Commandant Piłsudski himself, for his bravura in the war against the Soviet Union in 1920. He received several other military decorations, though I don't remember what they were awarded for.

As a child, I knew these medals represented an important symbol for the past of Poland and possibly for its future. One lasting lesson from my father's stories is my cousins' and my own aversion to anything communist or Soviet. Most of my cousins became inculcated with these dislikes and never adhered to any pro-Soviet association during Poland's forced inclusion in the Soviet Bloc. My father's way of coping with the loss of Poland's glorious and promising inter-war period of the 1920s and 1930s was alcohol. He often drank, though never alone. It was usually with some colleagues from PKS (Państwowa Komunikacja Samochodowa [State Automobile Transport]) the local transportation company, where he worked as an accountant. After leaving the bar, he would take the bus home proclaiming to the fellow passengers that the current regime would undoubtedly die as long as Polish patriots like him lived; sometimes, he would intone the national anthem,

> Poland has not yet perished,
> So long as we still live.
> What the foreign force has taken from us
> We shall with sabre retrieve.

The passengers who knew my father tried to hide from him to avoid any association with the reactionary rebel. If he had done this in the United States, he would probably have lost his job, at least if he was working for a state agency. In the communist Poland of the 1960s, paradoxically, a public rebellion was possible and often unpunishable. My father never lost his accountancy job. When drunk, he usually went to the cemetery to meditate at the tomb of my parents' first child, a daughter who died aged one month old, after an unauthorized transfusion of the wrong blood type. There was no accountability for such mistakes in the Poland of the 1950s. "Have another child" was the answer.

In one of the pictures that managed to reach America, I am about five years old, standing on the terrace in front of the "manor." Behind the manor there is a shed in which we kept hens and rabbits. These animals were my intimate world; I fed them, and I knew their personalities. It was the world in which, as my parents' only child, I found myself like Tarzan in the jungle. The hens responded to my care by running toward me whenever they saw me. They feared my father; at the sight of him they ran away with a loud clucking. Hens were enemies of his well-kept garden in the front to the house. Occasionally, they penetrated through the hedge and caused damage to the plants with their feet. If my father surprised the culprit, an artillery of stones would be projected in its direction. Hence, most of the birds knew about the forbidden garden and usually did not venture there. The springtime, after the last snow and ice melted, caused a great agitation in the menagerie. Either a broody hen was hatching eggs or my mother bought chicks from an artificial hatchery. In any case, the chicks needed to be kept in our kitchen until they grew more independent. That was a happy time, as if a sibling had been added to the household. Mother was highly relieved, however, when it was time to transfer them to the shed—their presence in the house gradually became more and more detectable through the sense of smell. Spring was also the time to put male rabbits and female rabbits in the same cage so that there would be a new generation for consumption. Don't imagine that the animals in our menagerie were treated as pets. They were primarily bred for meat and eggs. In Europe, rabbit meat is a delicacy. There were, however, exceptional individuals among both the rabbits and chickens that were spared on my request; these ones did enjoy special treatment as pets.

The most memorable case was a white-feathered rooster. He would let me sit him still on a chair and mimic the movements of my head. Unfortunately, one afternoon, when I came home for lunch, my godfather and a few friends of his were there for an impromptu visit. I was brutally informed that Mother had slaughtered my rooster for lack of anything else to put on the guest table. I ran away angry, in defiance of the indifference of the adult world toward my own intimate Arcadian space.

My undisturbed utopia, my world surrounded by creatures that had no malice and who reciprocated friendship, lasted for about my first ten years. The major disturbance of the idyllic order came on the day when my father collapsed watching a game on the communal soccer field and was taken to the hospital. I found my mother crying in an armchair. For the first time she had no solution for what was to happen. She simply said, while sobbing, that my father might not be back. He died later that day.

This close encounter with death was a brutal entry into the mystery of life. Strangely, my parents' marriage must have been a good arrangement despite the age gap. She hadn't married an older man because she did not have any choice. Quite to the contrary, she had had a fiancé who died from tuberculosis right after the war. She had kept in touch with his sister who lived not very far. I gathered that agreeing to marry my father was a contract of freedom. Remembering snippets of comments my mother occasionally made about the caring personality of the man whom she lost to the terrible disease, I inferred that there was no other man of their age, who would match his human qualities. She certainly did not look for average men who would make a devout housewife of her—she would have suffocated in such a relationship. Marrying an older man, who was worldly and educated, and who also had to do more than her to make the marriage work, had unquestionable benefits; she had the upper hand in any decisions made about the household and any life choices. My father occasionally complained about his powerlessness in his marriage to the younger Mrs. Motykowa, but clearly did not mind this arrangement. In fact, he appreciated my mother's resourceful practicality as much as the villagers did.

But that late summer day, the 25-year-long marriage was suddenly terminated. At 40-something, my mother entered the world of widowhood facing the challenges and traps of this new condition. By that time, she had become the school principal, a role she really did not like, as she was faced with constant absences of teachers on medical leaves as well as growing pressures from apparatchiks of the communist party (PZPR) to become a member, which she rejected firmly. Moreover, my parents had been lured into taking a financial grant for housing for teachers with the purpose of building a house. As it happens, the cost soon exceeded the means my parents had at their disposal. So, the construction stopped. The death of my father showed how much the marriage represented an emotional stability for my mother despite the age difference. With his old school work ethic, he had tirelessly helped my mother with all chores, and, in particular, the school principal's paperwork, which she did not like doing. And ultimately, after retiring from his job at the PKS when I was about seven, he had been a permanent presence in the house; my mother was not made for solitude.

Given my mother's insurmountable need for human presence, the real turmoil entered our life following my father's death. Faced with loneliness, a lack of money, and harassment from the party to become a member in order to keep the principal's job, mother started feeling trapped in this situation. For me, the pastoral landscape of my childhood was gone by this time. There was no time any more for the menagerie: Hens disappeared, while rats penetrated the rabbit cages and destroyed the brood. My childhood was chased away from me by the brutality of the world, abandoning me to the unknown. The only lifeboat I could cling to at that dramatic moment was my naïve faith. I am looking at my first communion picture remembering the moment when it was taken by a professional photographer and our pastor was exhorting me to smile, which I did only on the second take when standing next to him. My first communion was, in fact, the first powerful ritual of initiation that opened the door to the realm of spirituality. My parents were practicing Christians, but what helped their fidelity to the Church was the fact that religion was a fruit forbidden by the official government. The Church was the only institution that survived the war and the first postwar persecutions, particularly during the Stalinist period.[1] As I recall, my father's faith was probably more mystical than my mother's; she treated it as a matter of commandment more than a mystical need. Faith alone without human presence would not be enough to install peace in her heart.

I learned the sign of the cross from my nanny, a simple country woman. She also taught me a few prayers such as "Hail Mary" and "Our Father," or "Angel of God, my guardian." However, the true experience of the otherworldly happened only on the day of my first communion. It was an experience out of the ordinary: During the chant preceding the administering of the Body of Christ, I heard the words "The Lord Jesus is getting closer, is just knocking at my door" (*Pan Jezus już się zbliża, już puka do mych drzwi*), I felt a shiver in my spine that swiftly took possession of my whole being. At that moment I must have been marked forever by the imprint that held me together even at my most dangerous moments, always bringing me back to the instant of that first encounter. My confirmation

---

[1] On the complexity and progressive deterioration of the relationship between the communist government in Poland and the Catholic Church, see Roland C. Monticone, "The Catholic Church in Poland, 1945–1966," *The Polish Review* 11, no. 4 (Autumn 1966): 75–100.

ceremony two years later didn't have the same impact; my mother did not attend because of her latest experience of harassment by the communist party.

When the harmony of our hearth fell apart, it was the remembrance of that first communion that provided me with a sense of grounding. The consecrated bread must have been that seed planted in my heart, the heart in Pascal's conception, a gift of intuition that has helped me throughout my life to dismiss any attempts of darkness to kill hope. Pascal claims that we can apprehend the truth first through the heart, a sensory intuition closely connected to the body. It precedes rational understanding, which subsequently orders those phenomena that the heart perceives.

However, while the seed of grace was freshly sown in my heart, the enemy did not lose any time in confounding the new order of things. The forces of evil would soon act out an illustration of Jesus' parable on the fate of the seed in the ground: "The Kingdom of heaven may be likened to a man who sowed good seed in his field. While everyone was asleep his enemy came and sowed weeds all through the wheat, and then went off. When the crop grew and bore fruit, the weeds appeared as well" (Matthew 13:25–28). That divine seed would be challenged many times by the suffocating competition of emerging weeds, in the form of various temptations and trials.

CHAPTER 2

High School, Cradle of Fears

Faced with the pressure of power, the individual subject adopts a strategy of split (dédoublement). This consists, essentially, in that he has two alternative discourses, one practiced in public, the other in private. Public discourse is the very one broadcast on television, radio, and the press, which we hear in political meetings; it is the one that must be employed in all official circumstances. We use private discourse at home, with friends, or for any area that ideology does not touch too closely, such as sport or fishing.

(Tzvetan Todorov, *L'Homme dépaysé* [The Man Out of His Homeland] [42, my translation])

My entry into adolescence was filled with several tests that could have led me astray. But there was already a straight line in my life at that stage, following my encounter with living faith. Even at a time when my mother's world was being turned upside down, I clung firmly to that mysterious something inside of me that prevented a fall into the regions where youth lose themselves to the vagaries of human predicament, as might have been expected of a half-orphan.

Yet, without much delay, evil hit the core of my emerging belief that I was in God's special care. My distressed mother, having tried all sources to remedy our financial hardships, found no help and sought counsel with the new priest who had just replaced the one who had prepared me for the first communion. Soon after, the priest became a frequent guest in our house. My dislike of him was obvious. Moreover, the priest's bad approach to teaching religion did not help gain him any sympathy from me. Gossip about my mother and the priest spread rapidly. A few months later, some authorities arrived at school and told my mother that her social circles included a priest, an enemy of state education, so she was being dismissed from her position as principal. She took sick leave leading to an early retirement when the priest offered her, compassionately or cynically, the position of cook at the presbytery. It's impossible to tell if her dismissal was on the account of a possible affair with a priest, or merely because of her ostentatious contact with a representative of the Church. One thing came ironically to light some 30 years later in democratic Poland. A priest fighting for transparency in the Polish Church, Father Isakowicz-Zaleski, published the book *Polish Priests and the Communist Secret Police.* The name of my mother's protector figures in it; he was the chief spy for the region where we lived.

My mother's new job nevertheless brought some financial stability to our life. She managed to finish construction of the house, which we moved to when I started high school in the city. The transition from the elementary school where everybody knew that I was the son of the school principal, to the high school where nobody knew my mother, was indeed traumatic. I was shy, pushed around, and called by a first name I was not used to. My father had registered me in the official documents under his first name without consulting with my mother, who wanted me to have the first name suggested by the nurses after my birth in the hospital. So, in family circles and at the elementary school I had been called by the name given me by the nurses, and my father had accepted it. But the official school roster and identity papers always reminded me of my filial duty toward my father. In short, the high school roster was a beginning of the identity crises that plagued (or enriched) my subsequent existence.

Some of my cousins had graduated from the same high school, and, before I began my schooling there, my aunt created an aura of suspense about the difficulty of it and the need to surrender to its academic rigor and disciplinary demands. She was partially right, but it was also true that my aunt bribed some teachers so that her younger son would receive his high school diploma with the least effort on his part. She was determined that his young brother be less gifted than his older brother, was spoiled to an extent that, in my opinion, caused many failures in his adult life. I certainly did not want to follow that path, and fortunately my mother understood it.

I did not like my high school years, and I never responded to any invitation to high school reunions. It felt like a confinement with constant threats of some disciplinary punishment. In the Polish system, we had to remain in the same setting for four years. The teachers changed, but students remained within the same group or class. One positive aspect would be a familiarity with fellow students; however, a negative one was that there was no exit if you did not like your classmates. There was no individual choice of classes, and the curriculum was determined from the beginning by the administration. But I found it bearable and calculated that I should survive it for four years.

The students in my class reflected the societal changes Poland had initiated after World War II. About a third of the class was of peasant origin; this was the outcome of the promotion of social leveling by the state in accord with its Marxist ideology. That was certainly a commendable form of affirmative action. What the policy could not tackle was the attitudes of those from privileged classes, sons and daughters of doctors, teachers, or owners of small businesses in town; the latter were tolerated by the system, which they sustained financially with bribes. In fact, the cleverest of them actually flourished. These attitudes manifested themselves in cliques that were formed according to the members' social backgrounds and mockery of the accents of those from the countryside. I could oscillate between different categories. I had no peasant accent, so I fit into the privileged category, which I despised, and sympathized with those who, after school, had to go back to their homes and help with the farm work before doing their school assignments. I did not make any friends; I did not want to bring anyone home to notice my mother's complicated situation. I was uncomfortable about her demise from the status of school principal to become a servant cook in the presbytery. Moreover, her health was showing signs of progressive deterioration.

In this context, the best perspective to survive such uncertain times was to focus on a future beyond the confining environment of my teenage years. It was understood that after high school the subsequent stage should be college. My love of animals would have suggested that an agricultural major such as agricultural science or veterinary medicine would be a logical choice. To be admitted to college, it was necessary to earn a high school diploma and pass a selective entrance examination afterward. My cousin, the one pampered by his mother, had been admitted to the agricultural university, and my aunt, who had some influence on my mother, tried to persuade us to follow that path, because she knew who to bribe to secure admission. I found that prospect repulsive and decided not to pursue the option.

The field that overshadowed my love of natural sciences was French. It took over all the other subjects and became all-encompassing. It had the power to erase all the past and offer a chance to compete fairly with other students, because they had no previous knowledge from primary school to build on. I excelled in it. Was it a natural predisposition for language learning or was it a chance to uproot myself from my difficult teenage years? Perhaps it was both, in the form of an effort to find an exit from the old mold to the freedom that French was promising.

Hooked onto the possibility of applying to the university for a specialization in French, I continued to be the best student in the subject from all the sections. To gain admission to the French program, I also needed to be well-versed in Polish literature and the language. This was not a problem: I wrote well and knew my spelling—more than one spelling mistake in an essay in Polish would disqualify one from receiving the high school diploma. Participating in class discussions was more difficult for me. I dreaded expressing my ideas in a classroom setting. Ultimately, my teacher must have seen this and gave me an excellent overall grade. My shyness had its source in nature and nurture. I had a naturally contemplative bent rather than taking pleasure and energy from an outward display of my social presence. And, after witnessing the social and professional demotion of my mother, I had developed a distaste for any public expression of my ideas or positions. Moreover, I knew I needed to be careful not to express the ideas I had received from my father's ideological legacy, as they could compromise my future. To be fair, however, the political atmosphere was not too constraining. Our Polish teacher made a careful selection from the official reading list that did not focus on works from the so-called social realism that glorified social and political changes in postwar Poland. She loved 19th-century Polish theater and stressed its importance in forming and representing the Polish national character. We studied plays by three so-called national bards—Adam Mickiewicz, Juliusz Słowacki, and Zygmunt Krasiński. Their works dealt with different aspects of Polish mentality and responsibility for losing political independence and being unable to regain it. Nevertheless, the curriculum also included foreign authors, mostly French, such as Molière, Balzac, and Camus, for example. They became my companions: They dealt with human problems, avoiding the nationalistic tearing of clothes that is typical of many Polish authors faced with the incorrigible behavior of their fellow citizens. A universal human experience was the strength of French authors; more importantly, they displayed an interest in interiority, and in the human soul, rather than in a collective destiny that had been compromised or hijacked by corrupt individuals or external invaders.

Finkielkraut rightly underscores this aspect of French literature's contribution to world literature and philosophy: "*France is not reduced to Frenchness*, its heritage is not made up, for the most part, of unconscious determinations or of typical and hereditary modes of being but of values offered to the intelligence of men, and Levinas himself even became French through love for Molière, for Descartes, for Pascal, for Malebranche—for works which do not bear witness to any picturesque, but which, taking into consideration something other than France, are original contributions to universal literature or philosophy."[1]

That gaze into the human soul is the spiritual element that French authors might have inherited from their great tradition, which their revolutionary upheavals did not eradicate. My motivation to master French increased when I discovered the French library near the French Consulate in Kraków. There I had a plethora of authors to choose from. André Gide was the easiest transition from reading in translation to the original text. I was intrigued by his exploration of the self in *The Immoralist*, for example. It was almost shocking to discover the author-narrator's display of intimacy regarding his sexual penchants, and his struggle with the family grip on his desires and self-expression. The book showed me the antipode of the Polish literary landscape whose value lay in an author's degree of commitment to the national or nationalistic causes or collective political undertakings.

Even though the school did not excessively indoctrinate its students into Marxist ideology, the atmosphere was not conducive to sincere personal growth in freedom. There was pressure to learn from memory and to recite the material. Teaching methods, except for my Polish teacher's, did not invite much reflection. Instead, they fostered replication of the imposed model. The physical education teacher was known for shouting a chain of slurs at us in like the following: "If you do not perform, I will break your balls with chains." I suffered from sport-induced asthma and was not very good at collective sports but could not be exempt from the subject because didn't have wheezing as a symptom.

The failure of this system lay in the fact that its ideological foundation was false. As Weil or Kołakowski have suggested, the Marxist doctrine falsely assumed the ineluctability of the laws of history in leading eventually to fairness in the distribution of goods. I certainly did not notice any progress in that direction within the educational system that claimed its adherence to the Marxist "scientific" theory. Most of the parents did not believe in the progressive advancement of the historical victory over the class system; they just wanted their children to learn some practical skills like mathematics, spelling, and some sciences so that they could eventually become doctors and live well. Most of the students

---

[2] [*La France ne se réduit pas à la francité*, son patrimoine n'est pas composé, pour l'essentiel, de déterminations inconscientes ou de modes d'êtres typiques et héréditaires mais de valeurs offertes à l'intelligence des hommes, et Lévinas lui-même est devenu français par l'amour pour Molière, pour Descartes, pour Pascal, pour Malbranche— pour des oeuvres qui ne témoignent d'aucun pittoresque, mais qui, prenant en considération autre chose que la France, sont des contributions originales `a la littérature universelle ou à la philosophie.] *La Défaite de la pensée* [The Undoing of Thought] (Paris: Gallimard, 1987), 125 (my translation).

were warned at home not to believe in anything that supported the pro-Soviet policy of the government but to be prudent, at the same time, in sharing what they heard at home. Educated parents taught their children history by correcting the official textbooks and filling in the ideological omissions of information about the Soviet gulags, postwar exterminations of the opposition, the uprisings in Hungary and in Czechoslovakia, and the antisemitic purge in the Poland of the 1960s. Students from the countryside were possibly more receptive to the propaganda, even though the country priests had often tried to warn the youth against the communist ideology they might encounter studying in high school in the city. Tzvetan Todorov, citing Orwell, refers to this way of thinking in communist society as *doublethink* (42).

The school system was thus a paradoxical amalgamation, combining diverse threads that collided with each other, contradicting themselves to produce a rather cynical generation of citizens who only looked to take advantage of what was for grabs. If I had had a less complicated family situation, I would probably have enjoyed that period, as most of my peers did. However, worries about my mother's deteriorating health kept me withdrawn from the collective cynical merriment of my generation. I remained committed to maintaining or improving my social status through education, as a child of parents belonging to the intelligentsia class (as my father made me believe), regardless of its quality.

The Polish state school system was not even like the one in the French Third Republic led by Black Hussars.[2] Their efforts focused on a competition with Catholic schools in providing adequate civic education and, thereby, promoting a vision of the country as a civilizing political entity for the French territory and for the world. By propagating the grandeur of the French Republic, this education worked effectively in the service of colonial expansion.

In Poland, on the other hand, the communist underpinnings caused a degeneration in moral attitudes, manifested by a loss of civic virtues and a rise of self-interest and greed. The lucidity of Weil's criticism of the French republican school system applies, sadly, even more adequately to my experience in the Polish system of the 1970s. She writes,

> [T]he desire for learning, the desire for truth, has become very rare. The prestige of culture has become almost exclusively a social one, as much for a peasant

---

[2] Patrick J. Harrigan, "Church, State, and Education in France from the Falloux to the Ferry Laws: A Reassessment," *Canadian Journal of History* 36, no. 1 (April 2001): 51–83.

who dreams of having a schoolteacher son, or the schoolteacher who dreams of having a son at the Èole Normale Supérieure, as for the society people who fawn upon savants and well-known writers. ... There is something woefully wrong with the health of a social system, when a peasant tills the soil with the feeling that, if he is a peasant, it is because he wasn't intelligent enough to become a schoolteacher. (1952. 44)

That last statement sheds light on the social perception of physical labor in Poland, which is characterized by striking inconsistency. Rather than eradicating the disdain for manual work, the billboards showing pictures of super achievers in steel plants, for example, led to an opposite result. Mirroring society at large, the school system, at its core, was not able to infuse any respect for blue-collar workers. On the contrary, by officially promoting the power of the so-called pro-letariat, the outcome of the propaganda was a caricature of the working class that stressed the debased nature of manual labor. High schools had the requirement of manual work for the benefit of the collective known as "Social Action" [Czyn Społeczny]. In our school, it consisted of raking falling leaves from under the trees surrounding the school building during which peasant schoolgirls ostentatiously made every possible effort to demonstrate that they had never had a rake in their hands before; so much were they ashamed of their peasant origins. At the same time, blue-collar men, particularly those with enterprising skills, could dictate prices for construction work, plumbing, house painting, or, in fact, any services that required some artisanal skills. They could employ less skilled individuals as their assistants. This type of enterprising arrangement flourished and still does in Polish immigration circles in the West. This class of men formed a special category united by a strong sense of pride in their masculinity. When taking job offers, they dealt almost exclusively with men in the household, usually con-cluding the deal over a bottle of vodka. My mother was a woman and did not drink vodka, so completing construction of the house was a serious challenge. Despite providing a good income for this hard work, the blue-collar workforce was looked upon with vivid disdain, particularly by those with a higher education degree, whose wages were usually minimal or low.

The school was not particularly determined to stoke hostility against the Church. It treated it with indifference. In my biology class, we learned the coacervates theory of the origin of life on Earth, as proposed by the Soviet scientist Oparin. His boldest claim was that life must have arisen on Earth from the evolution of matter without any creationist agency, which fit conveniently with the dialectic materialism of Marxism. Since the theory was of Soviet provenance, most of the students found it laughable and soon forgot about it. So, the "scientific" character of the instruction did not carry any danger of religious disillusionment. My faith lived in the instant of my first communion and must have penetrated my whole being, providing immunity against the system whose ambition was to replace anything supernatural with scientific claims.

The danger came from the Church itself. This was not from the doctrinal teachings; I did not have any theological foundations to question anything and had trust in the Church's millennial tradition. The deterrent factor came from the attitude of clergymen themselves. The parish priests I knew culturally, intellectually, and behaviorally represented a living negation of Christ's teachings. Despite that anti-model, I kept going to mass. In high school, religion classes were offered in the presbytery of the main church in town. Only about a third of my class attended regularly because it was not mandatory. The priest in charge was not very charismatic or approachable. I would certainly have benefited from an individual encounter with a spiritual guide, but spirituality was not part of my religious upbringing. I dropped out of the religion classes altogether. It has been a mystery that, from the beginning of my conscious spiritual life, faith has never left me. It has remained alive despite a quasi-total absence of a positive witness to faith and to its moral content in those in charge of teaching the sacred story. I realize, by reflecting on its mystery, that it must have been the principle of "ex opere operato." According to Catholic theologians since the early 13th century, the term has been used to express the essentially objective mode of the action of grace in the sacraments and its independence of the subjective qualities of either the minister of the sacrament or its recipient. In other words, the minister does not have to be perfect when administering a sacrament to produce its lasting effect on the recipient. Surely enough, the priests I encountered in my religious education must have been seconded by the objective influx of grace because, otherwise, I would not have persevered in my commitment to the membership of the Church.

Looking at my early life in the Poland of the 1960s and 1970s, I see a reality that evaded the doctrinal imposition of its politics and economy. Socialism, which has some positive propositions of social change, soon succumbed to the corruption of the human beings in charge of its implementation. Ultimately, it was the human hedonistic bent that took over the system and destroyed it in its pride, seeing history as a theory proposing that humankind ought to march *ineluctably* toward fulfillment in a class-free society, according to the words of the propaganda.

In sum, I am a postwar child. My selfhood germinated on that soil, which had so recently been stained by the blood of soldiers, civilians, adults, and children of many ethnicities, in particular the Jews. These are my roots, which have given life to a spikey plant that stings at the first contact with its code of excessive sincerity verging on misanthropy. I have grown my spikes in a system that programmatically imposed deceit and falsehood as a main source of its power.

The Soviet-controlled Poland promoted lies about the prosperous perspective of the new political system as being warranted by existential necessity, and they were championed by the subservient Polish government. In a system of such permanent propaganda, besides the spikes, there was a need for a thick skin, a bark that would protect the sensitive interior of an only child exposed to the intemperate external influences of the political climate. A growing disillusionment about the direction of the country affected my parents' health until they physically declined at an age at which they still would have been productive in other political contexts.

Now, at the autumn of my existence, incited by Weil's thoughts about roots, I ask myself: Would Poland and its people have had a different destiny than the one I relate in this account? What could have changed the march of history, which Weil has identified with force? In Weil's analysis, Germany, led by Hitler, blindly embraced the ideological lie about the racial superiority of the Germans. German racism and its military consequences grew, according to Weil, through the acceptance of force as a supreme ruler of natural phenomena. She writes, "Force is not a machine for automatically creating justice. It is a blind mechanism which produces indiscriminately and impartially just or unjust results, but, by all laws of probability, nearly always unjust ones" (232). Hitler's Germany saw force as the underlying principle for building its expansionist ideology and enacted it with its legendary efficiency. Nevertheless, the ideological illness of giving force primacy in human affairs is not exclusive to Germany. Weil traces its origins to the Roman Empire, whose glorification of force prompted Roman conquests of the neighboring peoples: Rome enslaved them and destroyed their culture and religious practices.

After the victory over Nazism by the allied armies, the world judged less severely the crimes of the Stalinist regime than those committed by Hitler even though there were a few Western intellectuals who spoke up about the Soviet gulags and other means of repression, most notably Hannah Arendt in her *Origins of Totalitarianism*. And Poland was left to its new uprooted destiny, separated from the ideological family, even though it had been informed by Western Christianity for centuries, at least until the French Revolution. It needed to live under the yoke of the Soviet Empire. And my early life fell into that historical contingency forging my mistrustful character.

PART II

Uprootedness

CHAPTER 3

Kraków: Ephemeral Blossom

> Truth was the enemy of the system, but communism was weakening
> gradually despite its batons, and thus the truth could squeeze through its batons.
> (Leszek Kołakowski "PRL—Wesoły nieboszczyk?"
> [Polish People's Repub.ic—A Merry Corpse?] [78 and 81, my translation])

Searching through a drawer of a few memorabilia that reached the American shores, I find a photo showing me in a ridiculous, supposedly royal costume, holding the hand of a classmate wearing an adequately funny dress. It's a color picture, which gives it an altogether joyous accent. We are supposed to be the royal French-Polish couple Marie Leszczynska and King Louis XV. The dialog, to the best of my recollection, stressed the macho attitude of the monarch who essentially treated his spouse as a provider of his descendants while his true-life companions were diverse mistresses, including the most prominent, Marquise de Pompadour. We presented the skit at an artistic program by the students who took part in a French language summer camp at the Department of Romance Languages of the Jagiellonian University in Kraków. The year was 1979—all second-year students of French from all universities in Poland had to take part in it unless they received a waiver for having an opportunity to spend the summer in a French-speaking country. Most of the students did come, given the lack of travel opportunities. It was indeed an excellent idea to organize this program with the collaboration of the French Consulate in Kraków, which helped bring in native speakers of French, trained in foreign-language pedagogy. These instructors came from all over the world, bringing invaluable experience and fresh perspectives on language learning, along with a sensitivity to the Polish political situation, which was rapidly changing. This would culminate in a coup d'état on December 13, 1981. This encounter with the world from beyond the

Iron Culture was the happiest moment by far of my relatively short residence in Poland, as I am realizing when writing about it.

My admission to the university in Kraków two years earlier appeared to be the first major step in a liberating ascent. Even though my mother and I lived less than 20 miles from the center of Kraków, I moved out of my family home, given the relatively poor local transport. I found a room through a new acquaintance I had met during a mandatory one-month internship, meant to consist of manual labor in order to make university students appreciate the working class's condition. At that time, the disrespect for manual labor was already so high in Polish society, that this apparently generous idea was considered to be one of the absurd impositions by the waning political system. In actuality, it worked well, not as an ideological tool in the great scheme of progressing Marxist system, but on a very practical level. It allowed the freshly admitted students to make valuable connections. I was lucky to be assigned to do my internship in a dorm that was used during the summer as a hotel. I worked as a janitor. Some of my future classmates were less fortunate—they were assigned to work in the countryside in a fruit and vegetable processing plant. Notwithstanding the hard labor, they kept good memories from interacting with their peers, who they had just met.

My experience of being a student at the Jagiellonian University in Kraków was much more positive than my experience of high school. The university was proud of being the oldest university in the country and had a lasting tradition of resistance to foreign occupiers. These included the Soviet Union. A tragic episode from World War II was the rounding-up of its 150 professors by the Nazis, who sent them to the concentration camp in Sachsenhausen where many died. Most of my academic experience during my four years as a student was in a relatively free intellectual atmosphere. Even though my teachers were not explicitly rebellious against the political authorities of the period, they introduced their students to ideas from the West that had little to do with the supposed Marxist framework of the educational system. The program in French was probably a continuation of a program from before World War II. We studied the history of French literature from its origins to the most recent writers of the 20th century. Even though the literature study might have been a bit superficial—a lot of names to retain, with rather limited readings—it had the advantage of giving a broad historical perspective on the development of the French language and its letters. The stress was on language proficiency since the program essentially prepared high school teachers of French. Nevertheless, only very few wanted to be schoolteachers. Most of the students wanted to be able to travel and possibly to work in business.

The program had some general education requirements intended to reinforce the ideological framework of higher education. This did not work because very few believed in the principles of the socialist economy that was failing flagrantly in front of everybody's eyes. The course on Marxist philosophy was taught by a person who soon entered the opposition when it was legalized, under pressure from the newly formed trade union Solidarność. The instructor designed his course as a history of philosophy; Marxism was presented as one of many currents and not as a culmination of philosophical undertakings throughout history. The subject of political economy offered an exposé in wooden rhetoric contradicted by the reality of the shortages of food and basic necessity products such as toothpaste or toilet paper. After leaving the lecture hall, one often saw huge lines on the street in front of a market.

Occasionally one could hear someone ask, "What are they selling today?" The economic crisis reached its most severe phase during the preparations for the Moscow Olympics in 1980. The Soviet Union forced Poland to become a major supplier of food and other goods for the games, pretending publicly that Poland was in a tough international contest to do so. The United States (under the presidency of Jimmy Carter) and several of its allies boycotted the event as retaliation for the Soviet Union's invasion of Afghanistan. Nevertheless, the games took place, attended mostly by the countries from the Eastern Bloc, with only limited participation from the Western countries.

The symbol of the perversity of this "socialist" system was Pevex, a hybrid Polish-English acronym of Przedsiębiorstwo Eksportu Wewnętrznego [Internal Export Company]. Each major city had at least one Pevex. While the Polish stores were growing deficient in any goods, including clothing, Pevex looked like a Western store with quality goods that could be acquired for hard currency, in particular the U.S. dollar. The goal was to remedy the state's foreign currencies' shortage by forcing the population to spend foreign currency in the state-owned market. Poles received foreign currency either from their emigrant family members in the West or simply bought it on the black market. We usually bought dollars from a "cinkciarz," an illegal dealer of foreign currency typically active in the city center. The word comes from the way these individuals pronounced the English word "change" [cheenk]. Another name for these money changers was the endearing "konik" [little horse]. When I bought a pair of jeans in Pevex, it cost about half of my mother's monthly pension, but it was worth it because a pair of Wranglers lasted almost two years of daily wear.

The fallacious economic and political system could no longer contain the rising dissent. In fact, several foci of rebellion against the political status quo arose during my years in Kraków. One immense blow to the communist system was the election of a pope from Poland in 1978. The ascent of John Paul II to the leadership of the Catholic Church emboldened the resistance in Poland. On September 22, 1980, the independent Polish trade union Solidarność was formally registered. It was conceived during a strike in August 1980 at the Lenin shipyard in Gdansk.[1] Workers demanded wage raises and the reinstatement of colleagues who had been punitively laid off. Over a few days, strikes spread throughout most of Poland. Under the pressure of strikes, the government accepted an agreement on August 31 that allowed for free and independent unions. The agreement also promised freedom of religious and political expression. Soon after, Solidarność had 10 million members, about a third of Poland's working population.

I was in my second year in Kraków when John Paul II visited Poland for the first time in June 1979. I managed to attend the pope's meeting with the youth at the Skałka shrine in Kraków. The field was full and the atmosphere electrifying. One outcome of this encounter was undeniable; the years of the political system in place were numbered. Indeed, a decade later, the world of the socialist promise, imposed on the eastern side of the European divide at the Yalta Conference in 1945, was to come to an end. At Yalta, the allies handed Eastern Europe over to the political and economic influence of the Soviet camp. In 1989, the Eastern Bloc peacefully unraveled.

In the West, this impact of the papal election has been now minimized politically, due to John Paul II's conservative stance on issues related to sexuality and gender roles and simply from historical ignorance of Poland's troubled past. For the nations on the other side of the Iron Curtain, these were not issues at that time. People wanted food and freedom of movement and speech. Obviously, the Church capitalized on this election and rose to an unprecedented prominence in the entire country. The Soviet Union was very nervous regarding John Paul II's influence on the political development in Poland, and it is "beyond any reasonable doubt" (as concluded by an Italian parliamentary commission) that they orchestrated an attack on the pope in 1981 during which he was seriously wounded.

---

[1] On the rise of the independent trade union in communist Poland, see Keith John Lepak, *Prelude to Solidarity: Poland and the Politics of the Gierek Regime* (Columbia University Press, 1989).

It is somehow unfortunate that the impact of Karol Wojtyła's election to the papacy has been overshadowed in the West by the focus on his traditional intransigent stance on issues related to sexuality, such as birth control, divorce, and homosexuality. At the time of the revolt of the Polish working class and intelligentsia against the Soviet domination of the Eastern block, the issues of sexuality did not enter the scope of the political claims of the rising opposition. People wanted enough food in stores, freedom of international travel, and, ultimately, freedom of speech in the media. The Catholic Church benefited from the political movement of rebellion and staunchly supported its consolidation. Having a Polish Pope emboldened the mood of contestation in the country causing nervousness in the Soviet Union that likely culminated in the attempted assassination of John Paul II in 1981.

During this phase of an unstoppable process of disentanglement from the corrupt political system, I remained a passive observer. Now, at the dusk of my existence, torn between guilt and self-justification, I examine my attitude at the time, when I might have had a chance to become a political activist. I never did, even though I had received all the right political instruction from my father that could have prompted me to follow in his footsteps, at the first opportunity when the communist government was forced to recognize the opposition. I did not engage. I only applauded from a distance. There was a thread within me that did not allow me to take a decisive step into politics. In part, it might have been an attempt to dissociate myself from my father, whose stories of heroic deeds, often repeated in a mood enhanced by alcohol, had stirred rebellion against my identification with his image. I was not going to be a replica of my father even though he might have wished me to do so. At the age of 40, his military career had been over, first with defeat by the Germans, then later with the advent of the New Polish Army allied with its patron, the Soviet Red Army, which claimed to have liberated Poland from the German occupation. My father had become bitter and unreconciled to the new postwar reality. I did not want to be absorbed by his world of the past glory.

Reading Simone Weil helps me realize that this quasi-aversion to the political might be not such a bad attitude. It can be compared to her mistrust of ideology and the commitment to the truth that ideologies try to camouflage: "Idolatry is an armour, prevents pain from entering the soul" (217). My father's love of the Poland of his youth was indeed a form of idolatry that overshadowed any possibility of accommodation within the Poland into which historical contingency had thrown him. At university, I witnessed the new political behaviors. All the speeches and actions showing a new enthusiasm for change, for a better tomorrow, did not touch the right nerve in me to provoke a reaction. Moreover, my main existential preoccupation of the moment was my mother's declining health and the awareness that she would pass away before I concluded my education, making my future quite uncertain. My personal reality with a perspective of suffering, decline, and death was more pressing than the political transformation of Poland.

The enchanting summer in the French language camp was the last "happy hour" of my Polish existence. The French instructors left Poland, and we started our third school year in a tense national atmosphere. I witnessed quite a few political meetings on the streets of Kraków, including one with the famous leader Lech Walesa. As an outcome of the student movement, some of the instructors changed their attitude. It was not uncommon for them to insult students at any possible chance; for example, when a student gave a wrong answer, he or she would hear, "Mademoiselle (Monsieur), you are an idiot," or "Mademoiselle, you are living proof that beauty and intelligence do not make a good marriage." I don't think this type of authoritarian treatment had its origins in the communist system. It probably went back to prewar Poland. The communist arrogance might have reinforced it. The new times on the horizon caused fear in those instructors, who visibly changed their ways in classroom.

As the climate was changing, so was my mother's health: In addition to diabetes, she suffered from degenerative arthritis that attacked her hands and ankles. The pain was becoming excruciating with no cure available. I recall a medical visit with a specialist who had the reputation of being an expert in curing rheumatic diseases. She was also known for not doing it for free. My mother took an envelope filled with dollars; the doctor opened it before examining the patient and said, "This is lamentable." The specialist left us with aspirin for the rest of the treatment.

I contacted one of the French instructors with whom I became friends, and his family generously supplied us monthly with the medication Voltaren that considerably eased pain, although without curing it. It was a strange world to live in—on the one hand, a liberating move to the university that made me forget the stiffness of Polish secondary education, but on the other hand, a greater degradation of the reality that I could not leave behind due to my filial obligation. In this strange atmosphere, during the second semester, I discovered that there was an option to receive a scholarship to spend a month studying at the University of Grenoble in France. If it had not been the year during which the independent union was officially recognized, I would not have had the slightest chance to be selected, because it was public knowledge that these scholarships went to the daughters or sons of some highly placed dignitaries or spies. That year, thanks to the president of the student body, a radical supporter of the reforms, I found myself on the list of the scholarship's recipients.

A few photos from that study abroad remain in my personal archives. One of them, in the pale colors of a cheap camera, shows me in Venice next to a member of our expedition, whose father, according to the student leader (also a member of the group), was the chief of police in a small town, who was particularly active in tracking the political opposition. She might have been sent with us to report on our activities, but in reality, she too succumbed to the charm of the South of Europe, particularly to Mediterranean men who flocked to university campuses in France to look for easy prey in women from the North on their study abroad. Our spy was a perfectly typical example of these amorous encounters. She even dyed her hair blonde to look more Nordic. It took her only a few days to attract one of the men, who presented himself as an expert in computer science perfecting his knowledge in a summer study course. He made her a promise of marriage and then disappeared from the surface of the Earth on the penultimate day of our sojourn, leaving our Mata Hari in tears.

Tragicomic as the adventure of the policeman's daughter might be, it serves, nevertheless, as a stereotype of our collective experience in the West. The desire to belong to the Western world, to escape the communist gloom, or the Polish reality altogether, was the incentive for all of us who applied to study a Western language and culture. We idolized its alterity and ability to overcome the human existential *mal de vivre*, with which Western culture dealt by covering it up with sets of illusory substitutes to prevent the subject from entering the often-painful process of spiritual self-awareness. Simone Weil's judgment rings ever true when she talks of idolatry as an armor to protect the soul from pain. The idolatry of wealth and moral and spiritual mediocrity have been propagated by glossy advertising. Weil jokingly brings up examples of the intrusion of modern media into the life in the countryside. She writes, "Naturally, this state of mind is aggravated by the setting up of the wireless and cinemas in the villages, and by the sale of newspapers like *Confidences* and *Marie Claire*, compared with which cocaine is a harmless product" (76).

With limited access, we could savor those periodicals in the library of the French "Salle de Lecture" [reading room] in the city. They did have the appeal of an idol that makes one forget one's own condition and allows one to drift beyond the confines of one's human reality. Even before the subsequent shortages of goods in stores, Coca-Cola and Pepsi appeared in the delicatessens of the city where I spent vacations with my cousin. In those characteristically shaped bottles, which one can still find today in Mexico, Coca-Cola or Pepsi beckoned to the Polish youth, spawning desirous imagination about a world beyond the national borders just as perversely as Pevex did. Many years later, I had a revival of that experience while watching the Italian film *Lamerica* showing hungry and poorly dressed Albanian children contemplating advertising from Italian television in the store of the village.

The complexity of the inputs from that experience of studying abroad is difficult to evaluate. Was it needed? Did it work as intended? For certain, it improved our language proficiency and allowed us to discover another way of living. Yet, it undoubtedly made the return to Poland tougher. And the encounters with sojourners from other countries made us also see that we were enjoying much more freedom than our counterparts from the Soviet Union or China. Amazing reports from the Polish shipyards that summer of 1980, along with stunning photographs in *Paris Match*, injected some anxiety about the unfolding of the strike and its outcome. I confronted a group of Soviet students in the cafeteria when they asked what this rebellion was about. I quickly replied, "It was against your domination." The reaction came from a Soviet Azari, who told me how ungrateful Polish people were for all that the Red Army had done for Poland in World War II. Then, as if the spirit of my father entered my own, I retorted, "We would have been better off without. We want freedom."

She replied, "You want that freedom of crime and disorder like over here?"

"Yes, I prefer it to your totalitarian order."

Then she almost lost it, saying, "Do you want me to slap you in the name of this freedom you defend blindly?" The conversation ended there without blows being traded.

The ceasefire was helped by a fellow student from the Soviet Ukraine who told the belligerent Azari, "Don't waste your time. My grandmother was Polish. She never accepted the necessary victory of our country; she ended any conversation by evoking the 'Matka Boska Częstochowska' [Our Lady of Czestochowa]. These people are like that." While pronouncing the name of our Lady in Polish, I noticed a spark in the eyes of the student of Polish descent that probably contradicted the official censure she had to utter. The Soviet students obediently left the cafeteria in their ranks, supervised by their apparatchiks.

Encounters with the Chinese group were not confrontational. With a few exceptions, they all wore Maoist uniforms. They engaged in conversation with other foreigners without delivering propaganda discourses like the Soviet students did. I sympathized with a man who showed an interest in learning about Poland—we often had lunch together in the university cafeteria. The two exceptions to the uniform attire were two women from Shanghai. They seemed freer in connecting with other foreigners and spoke remarkable French, which they had learned without ever traveling to France beforehand. We became friends. They raised the question of religion, declaring that their atheism made them free to do anything they wanted without incurring the slightest remorse. For example, they could kill me, and that would be perfectly fine. Hearing this confession caused cold sweat to flow down my spine. Nevertheless, we corresponded for some time once we were back in our respective countries. Our mutually radical otherness was likely the point of attraction; we were curious to detect breaches of humanity in the armors of our distant cultures. I recall a Maoist calendar I received in one letter, to which my mother reacted with a gentle smile, proud of her son's international engagement. Poles have always had a weak spot for the Chinese. It is hard to tell why: on the one hand, it must be the exoticism of the radical other, and perhaps there is some affinity due to the common communist experience. Based on that encounter, Chinese communism seemed to me more organically grounded in the culture. There was a detectible sense of voluntary surrender to the collective ways. That surrender probably made it possible to act more freely in the world outside the parameters of the close supervision. By contrast, the Soviet presence abroad projected an impression that, without a close control, these individuals would have dispersed immediately and disappeared in the capitalist reality.

The train trip from Grenoble to Poland through Northern Italy, Vienna, and Czechoslovakia took a few days. We plotted an escape from the company of the policeman's daughter, who had acquired several suitcases of Western consolation goods after the marriage plans fell apart. She would probably have asked men in the group for assistance with carrying them. After stopping in Venice for a day, our group was retained in Vienna after a night robbery by thieves who shared our compartment. Some lost their passports and tickets. I had slept on my belongings and was spared from the loss. We spent several hours in the horrific atmosphere of the Polish Embassy that gave a temporary document to those without passports, although not before hours of interrogation. Those who lost their tickets had to buy new ones in hard currency for the remaining itinerary. My careful spending habits came in handy for my dispossessed peers because the embassy had no financial assistance for its citizens whatsoever. For many years to come, those who lost their passport were prevented from traveling and harassed by the police by being asked to spy in exchange for the next travel permit.

When I reached my home, my mother welcomed me; she had changed physically, looking more pale than normal. She soon disclosed in a whisper that she had been diagnosed with cancer but that it was difficult to know what the development of the disease would look like. This made for an abrupt end to a few years of blossoming after the dread of my high school years. The outside world was full of hope for political and social change in the Poland of 1980. My private world was going against the current of optimism. Fate had struck again. Why me? Did not my parents suffer enough in the system they had resisted with moral integrity not to have a glimpse of the new reality of which they had dreamt ever since the end of the war? Why could they not enjoy just a taste of the burgeoning democracy they had desired so much? It must have been an irony of Providence, taking pleasure in contemplating the misfortune of men. The story of Job comes to mind now—back then, my scriptural references were very scarce, as is typical in a regular Catholic upbringing. However, even without Job's reference at hand, there was a sense that things would go worse before they got better. Why would I have this premonition of reaching a safer shore beyond the need to go through dire misery? Was it psychology? Was I an optimistic psychological type who could not be reduced to an existential doom and gloom? Socially, I don't have the reputation, as far as I know, of an outer optimist. My spiky personality does not always make me popular in an ever-smiling California. The inner optimism that possesses me must come from an outer reality. There is nothing I have experienced in life that could produce this kind of life-affirming personality. Again, it must be the encounter with that outer reality that touched me in the sacramental mystery of the Eucharist and Confirmation.

These things did not come from my formal religious education, which was dismal, but a direct touch of mystery that made it possible to witness the squalid side of human existence without giving in to the ideology of hopelessness like many have in the prosperous West.

The last year of my Polish existence was to be a major trial of my resilience to the vicissitudes of life. The issue of *Paris Match* with photos of the strikers from Gdansk I had brought from Grenoble circulated among family members and friends. The Polish news hardly made mention of the events, merely calling the rebel workers hooligans. Eventually, due to agreements with the communist government, more and more information became public. At home, it was just a matter of time before my mother would be completely incapacitated. We thought it was jaundice. The hospital tests, however, led to a diagnosis that the jaundice-like symptoms were caused by cancer attacking the liver, and there was nothing to do but wait for the end.

My aunt organized home hospice care, employing a lady who my mother had helped to obtain a state pension and who was grateful for it. She remained extremely dedicated to my mother, which helped me continue going to school. I had a dilemma as to whether to interrupt my studies and be at home more or to go on and finish my last year of coursework. In a normal situation, taking a year off would have been commendable. In Poland that year, little was normal. Despite the agreements with Solidarność, the communist government was certainly not giving up its power easily. The discontent of the powerful neighbor in the East was felt in the media. Red Army maneuvers near the Polish border became a regular feature of the evening news broadcast. One day, I left my room in Kraków and saw tanks on the main plaza. I believe they were Soviet. Fear paralyzed my whole being, as I thought, "That's it; they have invaded Poland." But from a closer distance, the whole situation looked more and more like movie set. And indeed, it was—the Polish director Krzysztof Zanussi was making a film on the Polish Pope called *From a Far Country*. This came as a great relief.

Nevertheless, the tanks on the streets that year were like a *mise en abyme* for the events that took place about a year later. On the personal level, I received an Army summons to appear for my military service somewhere near the border with the Soviet Union in January 1982. "Run, run away," said the voice ringing in my ears. Several competing thoughts entered my already well-charged brain. "I cannot run before burying my mother, will she die early enough for me to escape?" The feeling of horror about the idea of wishing my mother's death sooner would come sooner was poisoning my filial attachment and duty. It was a dark night of the soul until my mother's death, my successful exams, and my purchase of the passport that led to my departure for France some two months after my mother's death. In the stillness of a dark night, I still had a strange intuition that light would break through eventually, and it was this that made me carry on through that year. What was the source of that optimism that could not deterred by the sight of agony, the political menace, the economic penury, and a lack of professional perspective? Looking from the perspective of my greater spiritual maturity, acquired through experience induced by the exercises of Ignatius of Loyola, I believe it must have been that sacramental gift that worked like a vaccine during a plague: a banal metaphor to conceive, as I draft these reflections during the Covid-19 pandemic.

Shaken, yet strengthened by the existential fickleness of the year after the trip to Grenoble, I decided to leave Poland for good. An only child with no parents alive, I had all the freedom I needed to decide the future course of my existence. The alterity and familiarity of France and its culture and language presented me with a clear direction in which to go. The main obstacle was acquiring a passport. It could take up to six months to get it. I had my army summons for January, so I could not wait. My aunt, who had extensive experience in bribing whoever needed to be bribed, came up with a solution. She proposed that we make an appointment with the chief of the local police [*Milicja*]. So we did. I recall a short repulsive man to whom my aunt, still quite an attractive woman, made seductive verbal overtures before he proceeded to interrogate me. I do not remember what he asked; it must have been a sheer formality before he cashed in the dollars we had brought for the interview. Until this day, when trying to understand the feelings of a person being harassed or bullied, I return to that encounter with the personification of the dictatorial state in front of whom human life had value only if it translated into submission, humiliation, and gain. It was an interview with a vampire whose all-encompassing power threatened my freedom and my bodily integrity and, above all, defiled my soul. The last element was probably the hardest to bear because it represented the betrayal of my parents' moral legacy. It added to the guilt of abandoning the ship from which not everybody could escape. But was it possible to do otherwise? Weil's insight on France's position under the German occupation helps to shed light on the predicament of the individuals who history had thrown on the wrong side of the Iron Curtain: "At the present moment, the United Nations, particularly America, spend their time saying to the starving populations of Europe: With our guns, we are going to give you butter. This produces only one reaction, the thought that they don't seem to be in any particular hurry about it" (92). This was the feeling in Central Europe at that time: The Western countries did not really care but had been calculating their own advantage ever since Yalta; even though they condemned the Soviet camp, they saw that it was in their interests to keep the Soviet Union happy with its territorial gains after World War II. So, I deduced that it was time for me to secure my part of that butter through my own enterprise.

CHAPTER 4

Paris: Voluntary Uprootedness

> For a long time, I woke up with a start. The details were different, but the broad outline of the dream was still the same. I was no longer in Paris but in my hometown…. My dreams never tired of inventing new variants to this impossibility of leaving again, but the end result was always the same: for reasons purely fortuitous, the return to Paris proved impossible…. I have since learned that this dream was common to many emigrants, at least among those who came from Eastern Europe.
>
> (Tzvetan Todorov, *L'Homme dépaysé* [The Man Out of His Homeland] [1–12, my translation])

I woke up in a flat in Paris's Latin Quarter, frightened by the dream in which I had not been able to embark on the plane as the airport was too crowded. The plane had taken off; I had had to present my passport to the border customs, and they had immediately confiscated it. I had been on the train back to Southern Poland when, fortunately, the rising Sun's rays had woken me up, warming up the mattress on which I was sleeping on the floor. "Thank God, I am no longer in Poland," was my first thought when I opened my eyes. I had a place to stay for a month, having been offered hospitality by a young French couple who I had met in Poland by chance while they were traveling in Eastern Europe. They had promised to offer a short stay if I ever managed to escape. They were committed anarchists, believing that the world was bound by political, economic, and sexual oppression. As I soon discovered, they rejected any social barriers in their way of being. The house was open to similar individuals who often visited and behaved as though they were in their own household. The hosts respected my rather uptight demeanor, attributing it to the oppressive impact of both the communist state and the Church. They predicted a slow evolution under their influence. Their friends and acquaintances were interesting individuals despite their social and political convictions, which I then found shocking and now find simply misguided. One memorable encounter was with an American woman who declared herself to be a communist. I could hardly wrap my head around this fact: "Did I escape a communist country only to find myself in the midst of anarcho-communists on the other side of the Iron Curtain? Is that fate's irony, to bring me into the core of the ideology my parents taught me to avoid and from which they suffered so much discrimination?" The human element prevailed. The woman was nearly as genuine in her political convictions as Simone Weil. She practiced what she preached. She lived frugally, as I was to discover soon when she employed me to clean her apartment. She also had to solve her own ideological dilemmas: She told me she believed me that she should be her own janitor but was too lazy to do it. But then seeing my predicament as a refugee looking for survival, she gave me a short-term job for which she paid generously, and which helped me save and add to the $200 I had brought with me for the whole emigration adventure.

The American "communist" was also the first Jew I ever met; she engaged with me on the question of the legendary, and from a U.S. perspective, Polish antisemitism. I was absolutely unaware of this reputation and knew almost nothing about the issue. During my schooling in Poland, the question had never been raised. At home my parents avoided the topic altogether, mentioning only occasionally what had happened at Auschwitz. My father was more familiar with prewar Jewish culture and often evoked, after a few glasses of vodka, a Jewish military doctor in his regiment. According to his tale, the doctor was a funny individual, who spoke with a pronounced accent and was highly resourceful regarding food provisions for the soldiers. It must have been that relationship that caused my father's enthusiastic support for Israeli attacks for the Israeli-Arab war in 1967. He remained riveted to the TV screen applauding the victors of the conflict shouting, "The Jews know how to fight, they will help the world to defeat the Bolsheviks by destroying their Arab allies." The following year, in reprisals, the Polish Communist Party declared thousands of Jews in Poland enemies of the state and forced them to leave Poland. The direct cause of the purge was the nationwide student protests when the Polish censorship decided to shut down the presentation of a play by Adam Mickiewicz, Poland's national poet. Protests were quickly spreading across the country. Given that many student protesters and professors were of Jewish heritage, the communist authorities used this fact as a pretext to purge them from the country's public life.

In one of his essays, "For Brotherhood or for Destruction,"[1] Kołakowski draws a distinction between two types of anarchists: loving ones and hating ones. The loving type dreams about universal human brotherhood, trying to give witness in their life to that conviction. The second category dreams about the destruction of the world they hate for psychological reasons. Loving anarchists believe that humankind may not survive without universal brotherhood. Hating ones would not discard the totalitarian use of force to destroy existing forms of reality, with no concern for what might succeed the destruction. In conceiving their means of achieving their goal, they are very close to communists, who anticipate revolution as a stage in building a new society. From this perspective, my American acquaintances and my French hosts were loving anarchists seeking universal brotherhood rather than hating ones seeking destruction. They knew that the world was not fair, but in their Western democratic comfort, they limited their protest to a certain minimum of engagement, mostly by sipping wine in the Quartier Latin and ruminating on received ideas about need for change in the world. Thanks to their dislike of the status quo and love for the world to come, I had four weeks of peace of mind before figuring out where to go next.

One day my hosts told me that it would be interesting for me to go to a meeting of the local chapter of the French Communist Party to learn about true communism and to hear various proposals of how to remedy the current situation, because my vision of the system had been deformed by the corrupted version of it in the Eastern Bloc. The meeting had an even more shocking impact on me than my encounters with people with communist convictions whose charm and human qualities overshadowed the dire ideology that I thought I just had left behind. I was introduced at the meeting as a refugee from Poland who was seeking to learn about the correct form of the communist system. Bear in mind, this was the year after the Polish government had had no choice but to sign the agreement with the strikers in Gdansk. I recall well-dressed French women who did not look like those stereotypically vulgar and tastelessly dressed communist agents one saw in the Soviet Bloc. I thought not, without a dose of irony, how good it must be to declare oneself communist in an opulent capitalist reality. Why would they want communism from the Soviet Union to be imported to their prosperous land? I did not know the history of French communism well except that it had strong ties with Soviet propaganda.

---

[1] First published in English in *Times Literary Supplement*, January 4, 1985. I refer to the Polish translation, "W imię braterstwa czy w imię zniszczenia," in *Niepewność epoki demokracji* (Kraków: Znak, 2014), 26–27.

Reading Todorov's account of his own wrestling with the question of the French sympathy for communist ideology brings light and solace.[2] He offers an explanation why, after testimonies by so many defectors about the totalitarian reality of that system, many French intellectuals did not modify their political stance and staunchly defended the Soviet Union as the best political system the world had come up with so far. It ought to be acknowledged first that the French communists constituted a major part of the "résistance" to the German occupiers during the war while the other factions were either passive or somehow collaborating. Todorov evokes two names whose publications should have reversed the French leftist perspective on the Soviet Union but did not. These are Victor Kravchenko and David Rousset.

Kravchenko, a Ukrainian-born defector from the Soviet Union, published a book called *I Chose Freedom* in 1946. The book depicts the process of collectivization, the prison camp system, and penal labor. It was an immense success worldwide. The French communist press, in particular *Les Lettres françaises*, did not wait to attack Kravchenko, accusing him of engaging in a smear campaign against the Soviet Union sponsored by American imperialism. Kravchenko sued the journal, and won the suit, receiving meaningless compensation.

David Rousset was a reputed writer, who used to be a Trotskyist militant before the war and was deported to the camps in Buchenwald and Neuengamme. Incited by the Kravchenko quarrel, he appealed to survivors of Nazi camps to form a commission to inspect the USSR camps, which became the "International Commission against Concentrationist Regimes." He was also attacked by *Les Lettres françaises* and also sued the journal and won.

Despite these two symbolic victories and many more testimonies from the Soviet Union defectors, the French left was not practically able to reform its views until the fall of the Iron Curtain. Todorov offers a subtle interpretation of this fact. He writes, "Why could this twentieth century *I accuse* not be heard, why did it take another twenty-five years and Solzhenitsyn to dare to look the truth in the face? At any time in history, we hear what we want to hear."[3] According to Todorov, the French intelligentsia could not wrap their head around

---

[2.] On the attitudes on French intellectuals in the post–World War II era regarding the existence of gulags in the Soviet Union, see Todorov's chapter 4, "Les Procès Kravchenko et Rousset," 89–99, and Kołakowski's "Dziedzictwo leftyzmu" [Heritage of Leftism], in *Niepewność epoki demokracji* (Kraków: Znak, 2013), 35–44.

[3.] [Pourquoi ce *J'accuse* du vingtième siècle n'a-t-il pas pu être entendu, pourquoi a-t-il fallu attendre vingt-cinq ans de plus et Soljenitsine pour oser regarder la vérité en face? A tout moment de l'histoire, on n'entend que ce qu'on veut entendre] (99, my translation).

the fact that the victorious Soviet Union could possibly be judged and made accountable in the same way as the defeated Germany had been regarding its internal repressive policies. They used all possible psychological and rhetorical devices not to admit the truth which would ultimately have shattered their ideological stances. It would have required a complete rethinking of their image and allegiance after abandoning their ideological construct that stubbornly called for the ineluctable future of the world as a borderless internationalist entity. The strategy was to discredit the witnesses to the Soviet horrors by suggesting, for example, that they were not French, and they had an agenda supported by American imperialism. During the Rousset trial, one witness testified in German and was attacked for doing so: How dare he criticize the heroic Soviet Union? He had to explain that he was an Austrian Jew, and his family had been exterminated by the Nazis. One of the arguments for denying the existence of the Soviet labor and concentration camps was the fact that Hitler and Goebbels had affirmed their existence; therefore, the charge was necessarily false. Given the influx of eyewitnesses, the French intelligentsia had to adjust their view slightly. Unable to bluntly deny the existence of the camps and purges, they began to justify it as a necessary evil, which was needed to preserve the gains of the proletarian revolution. It is disturbing to find among the supporters of these beliefs prominent intellectuals of the past century including Sartre, Merleau-Ponty, Maurice Blanchot, or Marguerite Duras.

The party meeting did not make me believe that there was another form of communism to strive for, or that the people I saw there were an attractive group whose convictions were practicable or even genuine. I simply felt doubly uprooted: first by the perverted Polish system, then by the French naiveté or cynicism in denying the reality of what was becoming obvious, thanks to the unraveling of the Eastern Bloc in that year. The meeting only added to my dire discovery of a world that should have been committed to the truth of human existence but wasn't. After all, an independent democratic country such as France should have allowed the truth to shine, thanks to the freedom of its citizens to think, investigate, and discern the essence of good living. Where was the Aristotelian eudemonia, or happiness? These people in the free world were buried in the ideological lie they had inverted themselves by producing false syllogisms like the one rejecting the existence of camps in the USSR because Hitler affirmed their presence, or just cynically refusing to acknowledge the existence of concentration camps in the Soviet Union, in order not to discredit one of the major players in the victory over Nazism.

I had to figure out how to remain grounded after the ideal of free democracy touched the ground and shattered in contact with ideological reality. I was not yet equipped with the method of spiritual discernment one acquires in a monastic setting. Nevertheless, it was a deeply felt mystery that made me resist discouragement and prevented me from plunging into the self-indulgent, self-gratifying opportunities the glossy Western free world was dispensing at my feet. The months to come proved to be a major test.

The hospitality of my anarcho-communist friends was to end soon; I needed to move somewhere else. I reluctantly contacted the friends who had provided my mother with the medication and explained I was in Paris and had no place to go in a few weeks. The entire family responded with great concern and arranged a place for me to stay for a year until I would be able to stand on my feet. It was a miracle amid great uncertainty. This French Catholic family was rather traditional, belonging to a bourgeois class, even though its younger members had rather leftist convictions. I found shelter and a family hearth for the years to come. After solving the lodging issue, I needed to extend my visa—I had come on a tourist visa, which was only valid for three months. I am writing this during great exodus of Afghan refugees before the deadline for the withdrawal of the NATO forces from Kabul. The news from Afghanistan is forcing me to revisit the anxiety I felt facing the prospect of finding myself in no man's land if my visa were not extended, even though my position was in no way as dramatic as that of the refugees running from the Taliban's control.

I was in touch with three classmates from the university in Kraków, who were in the same situation contemplating their possible future as undocumented immigrants. We found out that the only way to obtain the permit to stay was to enroll in a French university. We presented our demands at the University Sorbonne-Paris IV and were told by the administration that we needed a student visa, and for that, we needed to return to our country and request it over there. We needed desperately to break this vicious circle. In the university hall, we noticed a student activist who was very loudly exhorting students to protest to the university authorities about the registration fees, health services, and many other things. We must have had a rather sinister look because we attracted the student's attention. We explained our predicament, and, to our great surprise, the student reassured us that we would be enrolled sooner or later. Our surprise was even greater when we learned that she was the head of the student union UNEF, which stands for Union Nationale des Étudiants de France [National Union of Students of France]. The organization also called itself "independent" and "democratic." In fact, it was hardly so because of its ideological affiliation with the Trotskyist movement and closeness to the French left, in particular the Communist and Socialist Parties. Nevertheless, it rose in importance after François Mitterrand, the socialist president, took office that year, 1981.

Thus began our lengthy trajectory to the status of legal immigrants in France. The Sorbonne, whose administration was right wing according to the UNEF, kept rejecting our demands, which were presented with the mediation of the UNEF. The copies of my school documentation from Poland had apparently disappeared at some point. The tradeoff for the UNEF's assistance was our attendance at its meetings, which were strongly reminiscent of the meeting of the communist party's chapter: a stream of political jargon, bragging about the need to reform Eastern Europe's political systems, the need to bring real socialism to France, and the need to combat imperialism. By that time, I already had some immunity to this situation and was more able to brush off the rhetoric that I could not readily assimilate. We persevered hoping to be granted our student visa in time. The Sorbonne did not ultimately help, but someone from the UNEF had the clever idea of sending us with our request to the Parisian suburb, Nanterre, run by a communist mayor. And it worked: We received the permit to stay and to enroll at the Sorbonne.

Now a new chapter of our French existence opened itself to us: We joined the ranks of thousands of seekers for a residence permit. Todorov describes his own experience, "I don't forget the long, motionless queues in front of the police prefecture, where Blacks, Yellows, Swarthy or Whites like me, came to obtain or renew a residence permit, we huddled together to resist the cold and ambient hostility."[4]

As Todorov intimates, this was a collective experience for those who, at that historical moment, had been born in the wrong place under a tyrannical government and had come to the free world to find out, to their surprise, that it did not really want them there. In France, there were many reasons for this "unwelcoming welcome." Obviously, the roots of the hostility lay in major part in the postcolonial heritage. The metropolis attracts many nationals from France's former colonies. They know the language well enough to hope to find a place in the economy of the former colonial master. They meet with a hostile reception,

---

[4] [Je n'oublie pas les longues queues immobiles devant la préfecture de police, où, Noirs, Jaunes, Basanés ou Blancs comme moi, venus obtenir ou renouveler une carte de séjour, nous nous serrions les uns contre les autres pour résister au froid et à l'hostilité ambiante] (122, my translation).

shown with no ambiguity by the employees of different administrative offices, most notably the prefecture. Todorov subtly analyzes this phenomenon. Currently, republican law prohibits an outward expression of racism, relegating the racist discourse to a sphere of litotes aiming to assuage the impact of the words, for example, in the statement "I am not a racist, but those who refuse to surrender to our customs should depart," which really means "we don't want you around, you are not one of us."

The current international context, according to Todorov, exasperates the tension around the issue of diversity. Europe as a continent has dealt quite well with the neighboring countries, given the legacy of World War II. However, in the long term, the existence and expansion of the European Union intensify identity fears on the Old Continent. The traditional national identities are confronted with the rising presence of diverse cultural elements in the social fabric of the state. Back in the 1980s, the colonial past represented by the influx of immigrants with very distinct customs and visible racial differences caused anxiety about how to incorporate these newcomers into the social and political life of the country. The 21st century will expose the mistakes of the belief that the Other can be simply assimilated into the civilization of a culturally superior state. While France has been dealing extensively with the question of wartime collaboration under the Vichy government, the collective consciousness has repressed the colonial episode that lasted far longer than the Vichy regime. This repression is not helpful for the rise of a new national identity. In fact, it promotes segregation and hampers social and economic integration. Despite the sets of laws allowing the presence of immigrants in the country, the repressed collective consciousness of the democratic nation, and its fear of difference, led uncontrollably to the creation of monocultural suburbs and ghettos where anger and resentment toward the metropolitan majority dominates the cultural expression of these communities.

I had one advantage among the crowd queuing for the residence permit: I was a European, from a country that has historically had the sympathy of the French. My country has never been at war with France but was always its ally, and even Napoleon created a questionable legend as the liberator of Poland during his disastrous campaign against Russia. And ultimately, and probably most importantly, physically, I could melt into the crowd more readily than someone from North or Central Africa.

The help I received from the communist party added to my whole sense of uprootedness. I was no longer sure what to believe and who to trust. The France I knew from its reputation in Poland did not really exist. The communism I had learned to discard through my family upbringing appeared to be my most efficacious benefactor apart from the French family who offered me a shelter. The Catholic Church in France seemed to be weak and depleted compared to any strengths that the Polish Church had in a communist country. The churches in Poland were full, whereas in France, at masses, one could barely count a few elderly parishioners who would provide a lifeline to the Church's existence. I tried a Polish parish in Paris, which was much better attended, although by diverse social categories of people I was not familiar with: Most of them didn't speak French, so they formed a closed community for whom the church was predominantly a meeting place to make acquaintances, to see how to get papers, to find a job paid under the table, and to send goods to Poland. The spiritual dimension was not visible. I needed to disentangle the confusion in which I had placed myself by accepting to leave Poland and settle in the land of freedom. God was hiding himself for the time being, but he refused to let me go.

Paris inevitably caused a deep existential crisis in me. I began to realize that the social political reality of the Polish totalitarian or semi-totalitarian system had made of me a product that could not readily function in a system that required autonomy of thought and, above all, action. The structures into which I integrated myself were holding firm against the new elasticity of a system that required quick decision-making, providing for oneself, and negotiating multiple choices. Freedom revealed itself to be almost unbearable in the way it bombarded the self with a proliferation of diverse options. Until my arrival in Paris, I had lived in passive opposition to the governing system. Having been instructed at home, I saw the world in black-and-white terms. Good belonged to the past, and evil was the widespread contemporary political reality. In an ironic fashion, totalitarianism had dulled in me the capacity to see the world as a confluence of impulses that could be good or bad depending on how one applied them in each situation. The crisis lasted for almost a year. Looking back at that time, I am ever more appreciative for my French friends who must have understood the depth of that identity crisis and watched over me discreetly by providing a means of subsistence.

Not until recently was I able to label the phenomenon many nationals of a totalitarian system experience once they manage to free themselves from the ideologically closed environment. Reading Simone Weil, Tzvetan Todorov, and Józef Tischner, I found converging elements in their attempts to define the state of mind of peoples brought up in oppressive political contexts. Weil names this process of clouding one's critical sensitivity to the political real as the mechanism of spiritual and mental oppression[5] and dates it to the struggles of the Catholic Church with heresy that led to the foundation of the tribunal of the Inquisition in the late Middle Ages. Weil evokes the attitude of Thomas Aquinas regarding adherence to the Church's teachings. Neophytes wanting to accept membership of the Church were expected to accept all her doctrinal teaching at the risk of anathema. They had no capacity to become thoroughly acquainted with all the articles of "strict faith" yet must surrender unconditionally to the authority that had issued them. Secular political parties embrace a similar attitude toward their members. Potential members surrender their thought to the positions of the party they might neither understand nor fully accept. As a result of these pressures, the subjects lose their innate capacity to discern the truth. She writes, "Thus, the inner light of evidence, that faculty of discernment bestowed on the human soul from above as a response to the desire for truth, is discarded, condemned to servile tasks, such as making additions, excluded from all research relating to the spiritual destiny of man. The motive of thought is no longer the unconditioned, undefined desire for truth, but the desire for conformity with a predetermined teaching."[6]

The Polish theologian, Józef Tischner, writing after the fall of the Iron Curtain, used the term *homo sovieticus*, coined by the Soviet sociologist Alexander Zinoviev, to offer an analysis of the impact of the Soviet indoctrination on the psyche of the citizens of the country dominated by Soviet imperialism. According to Tischner,[7] totalitarianism wanted above all to spread a way of thinking to the people that would eventually align itself with the thinking of the political power. One of the most celebrated theses of Marxism propagates the belief that the ultimate criterion of truth is practice. Hence, it is necessary to frame experiments in such a way that they should prove the only true theory, which is Marxist teachings. The system based on such an axiom would not shy away from coercion to legitimize its claim. This assumption led necessarily to the "political lie." A very obvious example of the political lie was the statement that

---

[5] le mécanisme d'oppression spirituelle et mentale (*Note sur la suppression générale des partis politiques Note on the general abolition of political parties* [Note on the general abolition of political parties]) (Paris: L'Herne, 2014), 37–39.

[6] Ainsi la lumière intérieure de l'évidence, cette faculté de discernement accordée d'en haut à l'âme humaine comme réponse au désir de vérité, est mise au rebut, condamnée aux tâches serviles, comme de faire des additions, exclue de toutes les recherches relatives à la destinée spirituelle de l'homme. Le mobile de la pensée n'est plus le désir inconditionné, non défini, de la vérité, mais le désir de la conformité avec un enseignement établi d'avance (*Note*, 38–39, my translation).

[7] Józef Tischner, *Nieszczęsny dar wolności* [The Unfortunate Gift of Freedom] (Kraków: Znak, 1998), 31–32.

in socialism there was no political opposition and that whoever contested that "truth" belonged in a mental institution where they would be treated adequately to abandon their conviction. Language was not used to describe reality but to create it. Marxism wanted philosophers not to explain the world but to change it through the rhetorical means of its propaganda and the use of force against resistance to putting it into practice.

We find a similar analysis in Todorov's description of one appeal of totalitarianism to the individual psyche (36–37). Totalitarian ideology proposed the image of a better society and incited its citizens to aspire to it: "Isn't the desire to transform the world in the name of an ideal an integral part of human identity?" Many adhered to the propaganda image and helped enforce the construction of the system. This social engineering fostered the joy of having power over others. As the outcome, totalitarian society, contrary to its egalitarian claims, was divided into several groups in a hierarchical arrangement: on the top the party, the state, the police, and the army; in the middle, the masses suffering the inconveniences of the system (provoked by the economic flaws that eventually helped its demise); and, at the bottom, the enemies of the state, real or just those suspected of insubordination. Paradoxically, this society, like any free democratic society, encouraged personal ambitions and competition. The game's rules were radically different, nonetheless. Two guiding principles dominated the climb: the degree of servility toward hierarchical superiors and the degree of denunciation of the others. Thus, the entire society was under control. I need to mention that Todorov focuses on the situation in his native Bulgaria, where repressive methods were more extensively applied than in Poland, though the general totalitarian framework applies to Poland as well.

In such a context, the ethical dimension of human conduct is severely undermined. Communist society deprives the individual of his or her responsibility. The decision belongs to the vague pronoun "they," Todorov explains (36). Thus, the individual citizens felt numbed in their ethical behavior; they were not responsible for their own actions, which were coerced by the indefinite but all-powerful agency of "they." There was a certain comfort in not having to make any decision or taking any initiative. This system of rewards and punishment led progressively to the creation of the collective psyche labeled by Zinoviev as "homo sovieticus." Todorov claims that an attraction of the totalitarian system accounts for a relative initial popularity of the totalitarian regime. This attraction to a childlike reliance on the authority of the powerful is felt unconsciously by a considerable number of people who may fear freedom and responsibility and relinquish their right to it. It was the appeal of the lifestyle that did not require any individual initiative to construct one's future: The government took charge of it. The submission to the political regime eliminated the worries people in democratic systems needed to face. Here the choice was made by the government.

The communist system's primary task was to build a collective consciousness that would dull "the interior light" of individual human awareness of good and evil and form a new self whose moral code would identify automatically with the authority's thinking and serve it voluntarily. It certainly did not work in Poland, given the breaches in the system to which I alluded earlier. Nevertheless, it had had a psychological impact, which I started feeling in my first month on free democratic soil. I was missing something firm to oppose or to relate to. The new reality was not making it easy for me to see what choices to make, or where to go with my life. The Frenchness I had constructed from the accounts found in books and glossy magazines did not exist.

Todorov's analysis of the essence of culture helps shed light on the challenge of my new beginnings in a new context. He writes,

> The human being is not limited to come into the physical world, like animals; his birth is necessarily twofold: to biological life and to social life. At the same time as [he or she begins] life in the world, he enters a society of which he acquires the rule of the game, the access code, which we call a 'culture'.... Culture has a double function: 'cognitive' ...; it offers us the way ... to move forward in the search for truth ... and 'affective,' through which it allows us to perceive ourselves as belonging to a specific group and to draw a confirmation of our existence.[8]

Once in France, I discovered social codes and symbols I could not read very fluently. I found myself absolutely disoriented and betrayed by this strange displacement of my position in the world. My Polish roots could not find any solid nourishment at first. The part of myself I believed to be ready to open itself to French ways unexpectedly blocked itself. On the cognitive level, the learning curve was very high. Although I was highly proficient in French, the subtleties

---

[8.] L'être humain ne se contente pas de venir au monde physique, comme les animaux; sa naissance est nécessairement double: à la vie biologique et à la vie sociale. En même temps que la vie dans le monde, il entre dans une société dont il acquiert la règle du jeu, le code d'accès, que nous appelons une "culture" ... La culture a une double fonction: "cognitive" ... elle nous propose ... d'avancer dans la recherche du vrai ... et "affective," en ce qu'elle nous permet de nous percevoir comme appartenant à un groupe spécifique et d'en tirer une confirmation de notre existence (128, my translation).

of the language needed more time to be readable. A Slavic accent required more practice to camouflage my origin. The cognitive difficulties impacted the affective component as well; I started resenting my host culture and my new environment. Little by little a spirit of rebellion started overpowering me. I could hardly see anything positive in my new surroundings. At that point, I must have reached my direst ever state of uprootedness.

Probably the strongest sense of cognitive dislocation I experienced was the study of literature at the Sorbonne. My companions and I decided to try our luck as students at the Sorbonne once we received our residency permit (carte de séjour). Our Polish university records allowed us to enroll in a "Licence de Lettres Modernes" (corresponding roughly to third year of a BA in French literary studies). The modules on French literary analysis, in which students were required to present *explications de texte*, offered the major test for our compatibility with the French way of thinking. The barrier between us was like the Berlin wall. French students inferred from the text ideas that would never originate in my mind. The exercise was not helping my state of mind at all; it brought my alienation to a new low.

I found a great deal of solace reading Claire Kramsch's study of multilingual subjectivity many years after that early experience of wrestling with otherness when confronted with an alien hermeneutical state of mind. Kramsch's study projects an understanding of and ultimately positive attitude toward the difficulties the language learner encounters at an intermediate phase of his or her language acquisition process. Referring to Julia Kristeva's "desire in language" (14), Kramsch elucidates the state of mind of those learners who confront resistance to the new language. The process of the construction of the new social identity in a foreign language can be named, following Kristeva's definition, "desire." It is the need to identify either with the native speaker (in this case, another person) or with another image of oneself. In both cases, desire is a drive of the learner, whose identity is at the crossroads between the native and the foreign cultural locus, toward self-fulfillment, that is, toward finding a tolerable equilibrium between those two competing influences. This situation necessarily triggers discomfort and frustration. Confronted with the meanderings of the identification process and experiencing threats of disintegration of his or her old subjectivity, the learner might attempt to retreat to his or her native encampment. Kramsch defines "the subject" by contrasting the concept with the notion of "the individual" ("sociological or political entity ... guaranteed rights and obligations under a democratic constitution"), of the person ("a moral entity whose integrity needs to be safeguarded and nurtured"), and of the self ("entity ... given to each human at birth ... to be discovered, respected, and maintained"). "The subject," by contrast, "is a symbolic entity ... constituted and maintained through symbolic systems such as language. It is not given but has to be consciously constructed against the backdrop of natural and social forces that both bring it into being and threaten to destroy its freedom and autonomy..." (17).

The French university classroom was a laboratory that dissected the constructed abstract Other to which I had aspired during the gloomy days of the "socialist" reality in Poland. When learning French in Poland, I had created an imaginary subjectivity that sheltered me from the subjection to the political reality imposed by the government. French culture and its language learned in an artificial environment propelled me to imagine symbolic forms that represented freedom and enjoyment. I adhered fully to that closed world that was not penetrable to any intruder. "Desire" for identification with that world of symbols inferred from literature and France's reputation in Poland now encountered obstacles. My symbolic universe was shattered by *explications de texte* that went far beyond the horizon of my expectations. I thought, "What do the French look for in those wonderful pieces of literature? Why do they infer meanings that, to my eye, are impossible to detect from the surface structure of the text? And ultimately, why do all the students project such deep unhappiness and gloom in the classroom? Too many questions to answer at this point of the struggle for survival." My subjectivity found itself on trial. My "soul," that inner part of the self in Weil's concept, needed quick nutrition at the risk of total self-abandonment. My soul could not find it anymore in French culture, whose imaginary symbolic values just collapsed in my initial phase as an immigrant confronted with material needs and deprived of the spiritual values that were nowhere to be found in the new landscape.

Disappointed by the university, unconvinced by the political stances of those who were helping me, I needed to reconstruct my selfhood. Despite the frustrations, I persevered in going to school and finding such small jobs as my new student status permitted me to take up. This process of subjectification was extremely painful, nevertheless. The company of a few classmates from the Polish university and their acquaintances eased the evolution. We all were in the process of finding our ways through the labyrinth paved with new cultural symbols, the deciphering of which we shared on weekends spent together.

On December 13, 1981, we all experienced a shock hearing the news that martial law had been imposed in Poland. Tanks on the street; brutal beatings captured by international TV networks; letters from Poland stamped "censored";

and phone calls preceded by a voice saying, "this conversation is being listened to." Unlike the other Poles I associated with, I had no immediate family to worry about. I usually received news from an aunt who assured me that in our entire family nobody was imprisoned; the major consequence of the coup d'état was the fact that they could not travel. Only a few years later, after martial law had ended, a request for a passport by one of my cousins was denied, in retribution for a relative who was a fugitive. What assuaged my sense of guilt was the fact that my cousin fell in love soon after and got very happily married in Poland.

Paradoxically, our lives as fugitives from Poland improved in France, whose government gave us the status of refugees with residency and a work permit. I certainly did not deserve that title because of my lack of political activity; I felt I didn't qualify to be called refugee, but it was convenient to have the new status. There was no need any more to beg for the visa; it fell into my lap from the sky. The life of a refugee brought more stability and allowed me to work toward a greater integration into French society. The period of martial law in Poland led some well-known intellectuals and artists to remain and work in France. Through a new Polish acquaintance, I discovered a small church near the Eiffel Tower run by Pallottine Fathers who organized diverse intellectual activities with the participation of intellectuals, writers, and artists stranded in France. There, at mass, I met, now an internationally renowned movie director, Agnieszka Holland, and a popular actor, Andrzej Seweryn, who was soon to be hired by the Comédie Française, an elitist troupe specializing in putting French classics on stage. Occasionally, if the audience was expected to be larger, the fathers rented an auditorium in the neighboring church Saint Dominic's. There I saw the famous director Andrzej Wajda, who was filming his *Danton* with Gérard Depardieu in the title role, and Leszek Kołakowski, who gave a lecture. All these events helped us to remain within the high culture of our origin and go beyond the basic immigrant needs I had seen displayed in the regular Polish parish in Paris. Contact with this particular church nourished that hunger for the familiar during the process of transitioning from the old Polish self to the new self.

While having the residency and work permit reduced the anxiety for material survival, it also weakened my motivation to continue the study of French literature. What good would come from a degree in French literature for an immigrant who intends to integrate into French society? Perhaps it would help the transition on the psychological level, but, from a practical point of view, it made little sense, particularly as the study presented some resistance on the level of ideological approach. I passed all the subjects except one that required *explications de texte* in which my insights were judged "contestable." I then understood that the French really thought of themselves as a universal species who ought to dictate to the world the way people should see reality and have people erase any experience they could possibly have derived from elsewhere in the world.

This disappointment led me to look more into the possibility of getting a real job rather than wasting my time trying to fit a mold that had not been formed to fit my irregular ways of perceiving the world. The courses I passed allowed me to start the fourth year and complete the missing unit. But it was also time to find my own lodging and means of providing for myself. I found an *au pair* job taking care of two unruly brats. This experience did not reinforce my intention to pursue my studies; on the contrary, I began to seek a full-time employment. Through some connection I found a job as a manager of a small printing shop in a prestigious neighborhood. There were two major conditions attached to that employment: no studies but working full-time with an official contract of 30 hours so that the employer of this small business would not have to pay all the state charges. The arrangement was benefiting both sides; I was partially paid under the table but had healthcare and paid vacation; my employer saved money on the very high social charges in France for a full-time employee that were major factors in the high unemployment rate. My boss would often say, "We really like immigrants from Eastern Europe: you assimilate so quickly to our culture; you don't cause any trouble like those living in certain neighborhoods." Of course, he was right; on the surface, I was assimilable, although he did not know the whole story.

This belief was overwhelmingly present in French society and not only among the little bourgeois class to which my boss belonged. The philosopher and now a member of French Academy, Alain Finkielkraut, in his controversial book, *The Undoing of Thought* (*La Défaite de la pensée*)—published more or less during the period of my employment at that shop—gives the following appraisal of the situation in France: "It is undeniable that the presence in Europe of a growing number of Third World immigrants poses unprecedented problems. These men, driven out of their home countries by misery and traumatized, moreover, by colonial humiliation, cannot feel towards the country which receives them the attraction and the gratitude which, for the most part, the refugees from Eastern Europe feel."[9]

[9.] Il est indéniable que la présence en Europe d'un nombre croissant d'immigrés du Tiers Monde pose des problèmes inédits. Ces hommes poussés hors de chez eux par la misère et traumatisés, qui plus est, par l'humiliation coloniale, ne peuvent ressentir à l'égard du pays qui les reçoit l'attirance et la gratitude qu'éprouvent, pour la plupart, les réfugiés d'Europe orientale (131–132, my translation).

Like most of his countrymen, born and raised in French culture, even though his parents immigrated to France from Poland, Finkielkraut makes too easy a presumption about "the attraction and the gratitude" of refugees from Eastern Europe. It is true that the refugees from Eastern Europe melt more easily into the social fabric of France. However, this does not mean that they do not undergo a phase of rejection toward the host culture. Using a commonplace phrase, I could say that for me the honeymoon was over at that stage of my life in Paris. I felt deeply that the confrontation between Polish and French cultures reached a level of incompatibility that could not lead to any possible synthesis. How was I to find a way out of this cultural cul-de-sac?

Thinking about this question, I perused *The Undoing of Thought* to find an answer to the question of what it was that paralyzed my assimilation into the country's ways to which I was surely attracted and for which I had many reasons to be grateful. Finkielkraut confronts France's identity issues in the face of mass immigration from the former colonies; he asks the question, "How did we get here?" In his answer he builds his argument by evoking two poles in the contemporary culture wars: the Enlightenment and German Romanticism. According to Finkielkraut (14–19), the German philosopher Herder (1744–1803) introduced the concept of *Volksgeist* (national spirit) to counter the rising spirit of Enlightenment, with its universalist claims regarding human reason. For Herder, nothing can transcend the pluralism of human experience in each historical and geographic context. Enlightenment thinkers combated this attitude, replacing it with the notion of universal reason and ideal law. The leaders of the French Revolution attempted to implement the ideas of the Enlightenment by fighting national particularisms, defined as prejudice and ignorance. They advocated uprootedness from any particular cultural belonging in order to adhere to a universal human identity. After the revolutionary period and Napoleon's First Empire, the ideology of Romanticism coming from Germany took the stage in France's cultural life.

Finkielkraut points out that, ultimately, it is this heritage of Romanticism that was revived in the 1960s and which nourishes ideologically the process of decolonization, rehabilitating particular national cultures as opposed to the civilization propagated by the heirs of the French Enlightenment. The 1950s and the 1960s also represent a fecund field in the ethnological studies led by Claude Lévi-Strauss, in particular his work among the tribes of the Amazon. For Lévi-Strauss, there is a multiplicity of cultures that ought to be respected and considered as equal to any other forms of culture. He argues that Western civilization must overcome the belief of social superiority and reject the attitude of the blind refusal of "what is not ours" (Lévi-Strauss, *Tristes Tropiques* [461]; cited in Finkielkraut [72–71], my translation). Marxist thinkers of the 1960s and 1970s would add to this concept of class struggle. For thinkers such as Pierre Bourdieu, the predominance of a culture over others is explained by the dominant position of the class that formed it. Thus, as Finkielkraut suggests (75), postcolonial ideology might be seen as a fruit of the marriage of the ethnological discoveries publicized by Lévi-Strauss with the Marxist concept of class struggle advocated by sociologists led by Bourdieu. Postcolonial thought will thus argue that dominant culture has created the system of education that uproots and ridicules the dominated classes. It has two major phases: first, uprooting, and then dressage. In other words, tearing human beings from their habits and attitudes that constitute their collective identity, then inculcating dominant values raised to the status of universality (77). Simone Weil would likely agree with this analysis of the process of uprooting. According to her, even the French revolutionaries, with their good initial intention of freeing the masses from the yoke of the monarchy, failed in their project at the time when they proceeded to uproot various social groups, aiming to produce an ideal human model by means of "the most violent break with the country's past" (105). She writes, "The destruction of the past is perhaps the greatest of all crimes…. We must put an end to the terrible uprootedness which European colonial methods always produce, even under their least cruel aspects. We must also keep … some arrangement whereby human beings may once more be able to recover their roots" (49).

In "To Erase Hatred," a text written for the occasion of the celebration of the International Day for the Elimination of Racial Discrimination in Łódź in 2002, Kołakowski wrote—"The superstition that certain ethnic groups or races are inherently inferior to us, worse, or morally handicapped is the sinister, poisonous source of the worst mass crimes…. The diversity of cultures and languages, the diversity of human characters and skills create a great wealth of civilization, and it would be foolish to ask that all be the same."[10]

Who was I in the France of the 1980s? To the external eye, I was the grateful immigrant from Central Europe. Inside, I was an ungrateful, conflicted

---

[10] Przesąd, że niektóre grupy etniczne lub rasy są z natury niższe od nas, gorsze lub moralnie upośledzone, jest złowrogim, trującym źródłem najgorszych masowych zbrodni…. Rozmaitość kultur i języków, rozmaitość ludzkich charakterów i umiejętności tworzy wielkie bogactwo cywilizacji i głupotą byłoby żądać, żeby wszyscy byli tacy sami (in *Niepewność epoki demokracji*, 296, my translation).

immigrant stealing jobs from the natives. It was a period of wrestling with my own thoughts about a growing strife between my dutiful attitude to the generous host country and my disenchantment with its inflexible collective frame of mind, in which people believed and claimed proudly to be above all other cultures as a direct heir of the Enlightenment and the subsequent revolution. Such is certainly Finkielkraut's attitude in his book regarding the place of French culture in the world. However, for me, an outsider thinking he had anchored in the harbor he had dreamt of during his alienating high school years, it was the realization that my first love was only a first love and that it might soon end in separation.

My job allowed me to take a five-week vacation in August, when all true Parisians desert the city and go to their secondary residences in the countryside or travel abroad. Through the connection of the parish, I had met a Polish couple who invited me to join them in Spain, in a Polish émigré village near Alicante. The prospect of having a break from the French scene was very appealing. Spain appeared to be a healthy antidote to my confused identity at that time. There was a sensuous ingredient in that culture that was not coercive in the way that French culture presented itself. Music, dance, and food penetrated body and soul without telling one, "You ought to do it the way we do it." One simply caught the rhythm of a ritual and found it comfortable moving with the crowd. Many more vacations followed that first summer when I discovered Spain. I started studying Spanish and became proficient quite quickly. The phonetics of Spanish are easy for a speaker of Polish: Most of the sounds are common to both languages, and the stress is for the most part regular and easy to anticipate. This was clearly a factor in my swift acquisition of Spanish but not the only one. The subversive element of rejecting French was at work as well. My frustrated desire for French found satisfaction in betrayal; I had no reason to feel a desire for mastering Spanish; it came to me spontaneously. It was also true that, contrary to my aspiration to fit into the French landscape, I had no intention of settling in Spain; therefore, the frustrations related to identification with the cultural other were not impacting my attitude. It was only a cultural interlude, a game, but an important one that made me realize that I did not have to try to fit into the French form of life to find happiness; Spain revealed to me the fact that the world was larger than France.

The Spanish culture lifted my mood and allowed me to relax about my forceful and dutiful attempts to emulate the French cultural model. As it happens, one of the customers of the copy shop was a woman who had worked for the opposition to the socialist Mitterrand government's bill to cut subsidies for private schools under the state contract. The French education system remains quite generous toward the private educational sector (in which most of the schools are Catholic). It has a contract with the state which grants it substantial financial support, making the tuition fees relatively affordable. The French, in their spirit of rebellion against the dictates of the state, decided to do something about this. In 1984, French Education Minister Alain Savary, announced a bill—known as the Savary bill—to reform private schools. The new law proposed putting private school budgets under public control, considering private school teachers as "civil servants," and having the power to review private school procedures on hiring and salary. The National Committee of Catholic Education (NCEE) mobilized to protest the bill.

The activist lady enquired about my background; she felt confident that I would be the right clerk to whom she could entrust the delicate job of printing the documentation from the protests against the government's bill. I believe she intended to submit it for publication. Her request created another surprising dilemma; I had got my residency and work permit from the generosity of the socialist government, and now I worked for someone who was staunchly against it. Despite these misgivings, I felt that the defense of the private school system in France was the right cause. Marked by the experience of the Polish state, I considered any interference by the state in the private sector to be a move toward totalitarianism. That was one crucial element that overshadowed any glimpses of emerging guilt about my ungrateful allegiance.

Having heard my story, the woman replied, "Your story is pretty much my husband's story. He is Hungarian and he escaped his country in 1956 after the violent revolution against the Soviet occupier." This revelation made me react as if I had heard the call of the wild; a herd instinct filled me immediately, and I fell back on my Central European identity, saying, "We know better than these people in the spoiled West what freedom means."

Coming back to Todorov's statement about the cognitive and affective aspects of culture, I now realize that my cognitive relationship to French culture was expanding but that, at the same time, its affective side was growing distant. This encounter with the French spouse of a Hungarian refugee reinforced my negative affect toward the host country; I was grateful always, and respectful on the surface, but indifferent and almost resentful inside. The main positive lifeline to French culture was my contact with this French family who had an intuitive understanding of all the emotional upheavals a newcomer to their country might be experiencing.

The elegant defender of the private school system asked me one day if I was not too bored in my job. I said I sure was. Her two sons were in a private Catholic school not very far from my workplace. She offered to give my name to the administration in case there was an opening for a position of so-called *pion*, a discipline enforcer when teachers were absent or during recesses. A few weeks later, I was called by the head of the supervisors at that school and got an interview. The position consisted of working with younger pupils, grades 3–5. I was to succeed a young man who was "ecstatically spiritual, kind, almost an angel," according to the description of my interviewer. I was duly intimidated, but I decided to take the job anyway, which the interviewing supervisor offered me after setting the bar so high. Obviously, it was my Polish Catholic background that helped me to secure the position in a French Catholic school, but my sophisticated French was also one of the factors. Again, the irony of the fates smiled on my immigrant venture. I had got the work permit through the efforts of the Trotskyist student union, participated in their meetings as a young refugee who supposedly escaped the Stalinist system in quest of true communism, and now I was being hired by a Catholic school, the enemy of socialism and communism. My existence was turning into the plot of a picaresque novel.

The school welcomed me warmly. I learned from the school principal, a dame of a certain age from an aristocratic family, about the pedagogical approach of the school, which was called Ignatian. The school had been founded by the Jesuits. The underlying idea was to provide care for the whole person of each pupil by helping them to develop their natural predisposition and sharing it with the community. I did not have much experience of working with children; moreover, after a brief bad experience as an *au pair*, I was rather afraid of small human beings. But working with a larger group, surrounded by other adults, was much easier. I tried to remember how my mother had enforced discipline, which was helpful, but only to some extent. Here I was not at a Polish rural school; instead, I was hired to work for an elitist brand of schooling producing alumni of great repute. I ended up liking it greatly. The environment was more like what I had imagined France was. The cultural landscape was populated with more recognizable symbolism, which was more acceptable to me than the one I had been confronted with when hosted or befriended by the anarcho-communist category of French society. The recent events in Poland also meant that the teachers and the parents showed sympathy to me.

However, little by little, I came to the realization that this pleasant situation left little opportunity for professional development. My salary was minimal, with little prospect of a raise. I could only live from month to month and make a trip to Spain during the summer. I could certainly not foresee a family life with this wage and would remain Monsieur Motyka for the rest of my life. One of the Jesuit priests working at that school told me, in full honesty, that it was probably time for me to find something else; for him, it was obvious I could do better than this. He urged me to treat it as a trampoline for the next step in my life. I was surprised by this statement because, until this point, everybody had wanted me to stay in my job. He was the first one to encourage me to go because I was good at what I was doing. I found the priest's words liberating.

The job at the Jesuit school implicitly taught me the principles of the Jesuit approach to pedagogy. Observing the teachers, I learned what much later I could name as "cura personalis," a pedagogical approach fostering the development of the intellect as well as the emotional intelligence of the pupils, by teaching them to have solidarity with those less fortunate, express gratitude for what they had, and engage in theater to practice eloquence and rhetorical skills. When I found myself in the third phase of Jesuit training, called *regency*, a field practicum usually lasting from two to three years during which Jesuits acquire teaching skills, I understood that the years at the Paris school were my regency *avant la lettre*. When it was my turn to do the "official" regency, the transition was very smooth. I already had a great deal of experience in the field of education.

Of course, during those few years working at the school in Paris, I had no idea where this immersion into education might lead in the future. As time went by, I became bored; I stopped worrying about fitting or not fitting into French culture. One of my Polish connections suggested that we start learning English. There were many private schools in Paris offering English classes. We signed up for a course that was taught in a very amateurish fashion, as I can say now, and represented a rip-off financially but that still opened the door to a totally new world: America. I had never had any inclination to learn English, I did not like its sounds, and, despite having seen many American films, including many Disney productions during my childhood in Poland, I had not succumbed to their ethical message that good always wins over evil. By contrast, French was the charming thing with irresistible appeal that I wanted to absorb and to be part of.

Nevertheless, the encounter with Americans had a completely unexpected turn. The individuals associated with the language school were nothing like the Europeans I knew. They were a separate species. Most of them had come to France after graduating from college; they were on a personal pilgrimage, searching for themselves. Unlike their French counterparts, who, after graduation, were docilely sticking to the first job they could find, American temporary expats I met had no set career in mind at that stage of their lives. They incarnated something of the Great Gatsby, the hero or antihero of one of the first books I read in English. From my timid perspective of a refugee, they seemed to me like children on the playground who had the freedom to throw their toys away when they felt overcome with tiredness or boredom. They were generous and good-humored, but always ready to do what they felt like at a given moment or leave if they lost interest in a conversation, for example. They had none of the sense of social obligation that Europeans acquire in their family and school settings. This feature of American culture was both fascinating and frightening.

Now, I have lived in America longer than in any other place and am still in the process of understanding it. I believe I understood French culture and ended up truly loving it once I left France. Confronted with the American enigma, I have come to the realization that France was my most dedicated and most influential teacher of life even though I thought, probably rightly so, that I had no professional future there. For me, nevertheless, America was a platform of success in conformity with its reputation. On the affective level, with a very few cherished exceptions, my American relationships appeared to be fragile, not to say unstable or ephemeral. I was certainly attracted to the freedom of behavior my acquaintances displayed. This attraction even led to a committed relationship that eventually brought me to America, but once there, the winds of destiny changed their direction, and I found myself, like a lonesome cowboy, confronted by a splendid landscape with an ever-moving horizon like a Fata Morgana mirage.

But before succumbing to the temptation of the large, limitless horizons of freedom, I had this unique occasion to observe closely the behaviors of those children of the land of fairytales pasteurized by the master Walt Disney. The democratic American education created this free human being who no other cultures could produce because of their social constraints coming from the tradition and family values that are deeply rooted in old societies. It was truly fascinating to observe the freedom of these short-term expats in making quick decisions, establishing quick relationships, and discarding them, not being burdened by sentimental attachments or any other constraints of that type.

I believe Finkielkraut, inspired by de Tocqueville's account of his experience of American democracy, has pinned down the source of these attitudes: "Unlike all the listed human figures, democratic man sees himself as an independent being, as a social atom: separated at the same time from his ancestors, his contemporaries, his descendants, he is primarily concerned with providing for his private needs and wants to be the equal of all other men.... Such a rehabilitation of Western individualism would deserve to be applauded wholeheartedly, if ... it did not confuse egoism ... with autonomy."[11]

Finkielkraut is certainly right in his analysis of the justification of a selfish pursuit of desire by a sense of the entitlement to it in the name of individual freedom. This is the heart of consumerism of which America is the world's greatest promoter. Yet this perspective applies only partially to the Americans who introduced me to their culture in Paris. In fact, through their college education, they were probably intellectually formed better than any Western Europeans of their age. Coming from liberal arts colleges, they had good humanistic foundations and were open to European cultural influences. These interests were genuine and led to the rejection of American consumerist culture. In that sense, these young college graduates were a by-product of the rich materialistic culture that, paradoxically, afforded them the luxury to reject its core values. One may see here a contradiction of the American college education that, on the one hand, forms individuals who feel unconstrained by the social conventions typical of other cultures, while, on the other hand, this upbringing is susceptible to rebellion against the very culture that allows them to enjoy that freedom. They are rebels without a cause, at least to the outsider's gaze. From the stance of an Eastern European refugee, this rebellion was puzzling—my American acquaintances had everything an Eastern European refugee could dream about but were searching something they lacked. What was it?

None of them were religious, although they had a vague awareness of their faith ancestry. Some had a Catholic background, some Protestant, and some Jewish. Yet this generation was freed from any sense of religious obligation, as they were free from social conventions so important in European societies. Those from a Jewish background had the strongest sense of social propriety, probably because of their stronger connection with European intellectual and broadly cultural tradition.

Notwithstanding those differences, my encounter with Americans was an important phase in my intellectual growth. Conversations led to many discoveries

---

[11] A la différence de toutes les figures répertoriées de l'humain, l'homme démocratique se conçoit lui-même comme un être indépendant, comme un atome social: séparé à la fois de ses ancêtres, de ses contemporains, de ses descendants, il se préoccupe, en premier lieu, de pourvoir à ses besoins privés et il se veut l'égal de tous les autres hommes.... Une telle réhabilitation de l'individualisme occidental mériterait d'être applaudie sans réserve, si ... elle ne confondait l'égoïsme ... avec l'autonomie (*La Défaite de la pensée*, 148).

of intellectual figures I had never heard about either in communist Poland or in the self-contained French cultural context.

Observing the cultural fluidity of these young Americans, my sense of difference was strengthening, nevertheless. My awareness of the transcendental was solidifying in contact with these uprooted souls in quest of some meaning in their lives. Many times, I asked myself what was gnawing at them. They occasionally seemed to be depressed, as if the freedom they should enjoy was becoming an intolerable force in need of harnessing. Leaving the company of the Americans after a stroll through a Parisian neighborhood, my mind was flooded with a myriad of questions: "How can you be unhappy, you who grew up in the richest country in the world? You who could decide about your own destiny without any need to evade restrictions of freedom from the government or rigid social conventions found in Old Europe. You who do not need religion to preserve glimpses of hope for the future? What's wrong with you?" And then, wrapped in the inferiority complex of a poor Eastern European refugee, I tried to figure out what could possibly be the source of attraction for those Americans toward a wretch like me? Indeed, it was unquestionable that we were spending a lot of time together. As I reflect on this psychological deformation of an immigrant soul that tried to free itself in vain from ties to the land that had fed it in its early youth, I realize, after years, that my Polish upbringing had a strongly rooted stem that could not be easily torn out and replaced by a completely new implant; not even a new shoot could be grafted on the old Polish trunk, at least then.

Now I believe that the fact of having that thick and rigid stem was appealing to those whose roots had grown in a cultural sand of lovely beaches and under a permanent blue sky. They had an existential fragility that prevented them from taking unrestricted advantage of being born in a place where, paradoxically, boundless freedom seemed to be asking for boundaries, lurking enviously in places where centrifugal forces painfully strove to overturn oppression and censure.

PART III

The Graft

CHAPTER 5

America: The Unbearable Happiness of Exile

Still, there is a violent contrast here, in this country, between the growing abstractness of a nuclear universe and a primary, visceral, unbounded vitality, springing not from rootedness, but from the lack of roots, a metabolic vitality, in sex and bodies, as well as in work and in buying and selling. Deep down, the US, with its space, its technological refinement, its bluff conscience, even in those spaces which it opens up for simulation, is the *only remaining primitive society*.... Its primitivism has passed into the hyperbolic, inhuman character of a universe that is beyond us, that outstrips its own moral, social, or ecological rationale.

(Jean Baudrillard, *America* [1988], 7)

I moved to California about 30 years ago. The decision to leave France was the result of a growing intimate friendship with a person from the New World. It rekindled in me the desire to pursue my inner Eastern European urge to move even further west from the world of my childhood. This intimate relationship brought me to California and made the formalities of becoming a citizen of this enigmatic country relatively straightforward. But its unraveling has left a wound that may be one of the sources of my sense of being a *misfit* in the land that has been very good to me. In the pages that follow, I will explore the cultural challenges and the concept of sensitivities that do not translate well from one culture to another. While my experience is deeply personal, I will attempt to extrapolate its particular nature and apply it to a broader cultural and political context with the help of commentators whose experience of America coincides with mine.

I owe this country my social climb from the position of being a wretch with no English-language proficiency, to that of a university professor. I owe it a moral debt that is as great as the vastness of its limitless spaciousness. Since my first day, I have hoped, after years of uncertainty in quest for a fitting niche, to grow roots in this land of all promise. Yet my American roots are shallow; every year

I have to go to Europe to find some nourishment for my soul so that I won't wilt and be absorbed by the withered social surroundings of California. I have found echoes of my own response to the alterity of this culture in Baudrillard's philosophical travelogue *America*. He writes, "…for us the whole of America is a desert. Culture exists there in a wild state: it sacrifices all intellect, all aesthetics in a process of literal transcription into the real" (99). What I think Baudrillard is trying to talk about is the absence of that human interaction that this New World population might consider a waste of time, whereas for us Europeans, it is a vital play in which our human needs of closeness are met or purged without endangering the autonomy of our own space. For Americans, the need for literality in fulfilling their desires triggers the sacrifice of that social space in which desire diffuses itself into the mundane interplay we ordinarily call "culture." Our "metabolic vitality" is hindered by social obligations resulting from the tradition transmitted by the family and the educational organizations.

I discovered America on a rainy first day of April. It must have been a fate's irony to fool me in that land that I knew only through popular clichés and through my Parisian contacts with Americans. As I was soon to find out, this "knowledge" had little to do with the reality. The landscape itself had something enigmatic in its welcoming mildness. The legendary lightness of being, possibly a fruit of that clement climate, was hiding something grave under its tepid, mild coat of luxuriant vegetation revived in early April by the recent rainy season. The hills of Northern California's East Bay that received me with open arms but a half-sincere smile had an irresistible appeal for a former resident of the very urban Paris. The whole area seemed rustic, and yet it had all the advantages of a metropolis regarding commercial services. The hills, covered with fog or clouds, had an evocative power, calling to mind the Tatra Mountains above the Polish town of Zakopane.

The next day the Sun broke through the clouds, and the world changed into a bright reality dominated by a blue dome of a sky that I had seen only around the Mediterranean. If I had not had the good fortune of being a Christian by birth, I might have become a member of a sect worshiping the Sun. Even today, when the Sun hides its face for a day, I feel uneasy; it challenges my vowed commitment to the Catholic doctrine that does not support an attachment to any particular place. The Sun, this father of deserts, created by his love these vast spaces where thirst is never quenched. As Baudrillard points out, American cities reproduce desert in the way they are designed and in the way they function as social organisms. I am writing this page in Los Angeles, which the French philosopher summarizes as follows—"There is nothing to match flying over Los Angeles by night. A sort of luminous, geometric, incandescent immensity, stretching as far as the eye can see, bursting out from the cracks of the clouds. Only Hieronymus Bosch's hell can match this inferno effect" (51).

The Inferno effect of a desert city lies in the impossibility of it quenching that primal thirst for the truth. Desert opens up the possibility of redirecting one's attention toward the truth. But that truth can be only apprehended through a spiritual experience. The mystical traditions often regard desert as a starting point for a climb toward the reality that lies beyond the confines of the literality of its surroundings. European cultures have created elaborate social networks that mitigate the radicality of mystical drives by focusing on transient distractions: giving in to human passions rather than rising above their sentimental needs. In practice, social circles composed of friends or family members fulfill that mitigating role.

The literality of American culture that mirrors the desert, as Baudrillard suggests, makes it difficult to accept the elaborate, formalized social conventions of European cultures that diffuse the social tensions induced by human passions unrefined by culture. One might bring up here the useful anthropological distinction between the types of culture. The terms applied to denote that distinction are high-context and low-context culture.[1] American culture, to which Baudrillard occasionally refers to as "(un)culture," is a clear example of low-context culture. One could argue, however, that the difficulty of communication and the loneliness of the inhabitants of desert cities might challenge that easy division. The American behavioral code is much more difficult to decipher than the European one, where the individual, socialized to its high context through progressive intentional induction in family or at school, readily recognizes its signposts.

The so-called low-context culture of America deceptively impedes communication at any level beyond verbal interaction. What cannot be uttered should not matter socially. It is also one of the factors that encourage diverse U.S. communities to remain within their own cultural boundaries, because the culture at large remains cold in its naked literality. It is a culture of unsurpassable solitude. I share a sensation of shock with Baudrillard, who evokes the image of people eating alone, "Yet there is a certain solitude like no other—that of

---

[1] For the definition of high-context, low-context cultures, see Rebecca B. Rubin, Carlos Fernández Collado, and Roberto Hernandez-Sampieri, "A Cross-Cultural Examination of Interpersonal Communication Motives in Mexico and the United States," *International Journal of Intercultural Relations* 16, no. 2 (March 1992): 145–157.

the man preparing his meal in public on a wall, or on the hood of his car, or along a fence, alone. You see that all the time here. It is the saddest sight in the world. Sadder than destitution, sadder than the beggar is the man who eats alone in public" (15).

Fortunately, in California it is often sunny. As I said before, the Sun became my closest friend in my first days on the American soil. This is not to say, however, that I was not welcomed and provided with immediate necessities. The hospitality was outstanding. What was lacking was genuine human warmth, despite many embraces known as "hugs." I soon realized that the people I used to see in Paris could no longer behave like tourists; they were at home, and obviously their ways of being had to be those of the natives. Baudrillard qualifies that reserve as a form of fear: "They do not look at other people here. They are too much afraid they [strangers] will throw themselves upon them with unbearable, sexual demands, requests for money or affection. Everything is charged with a somnambulic violence and you must avoid contact to escape its potential discharge" (60).

In those first months of getting to know the New World, the most challenging thing was to accept the harsh fact that, to remain on the surface in this uncharted reality in this emotional desert, on these vast movable sands, one needs to learn as fast as possible how to walk alone, how to eat alone, and how to compete alone. My heart's interests soon revealed a great deal of autonomy that made it impossible to find common ground in pursuit of further communal growth. Again, I have recourse to Baudrillard's poetic and amusing rendering of American sentimental life to excuse in part my own responsibility for a failed romance: "Such is the whirl of the city, so great its centrifugal force, that it would have a superhuman strength to envisage living as a couple and sharing someone else's life in New York. Only tribes, gangs, mafia families, secret societies, and perverse communities can survive, not couples. This is the anti-Ark. In the first Ark, the animals came in two by two to save the species from the great flood. Here in this fabulous Ark, each one comes in alone—it's up to him or her each evening to find the last survivors for the last party" (18–19).

In this second Ark with its challenges to the tradition of marriage and procreation, I found, however, a springboard for individual growth. Alone, that's true, but one is also very free to embrace the mythical American dream. Compared with Europe, America in the early 1990s offered a plethora of educational choices for any pocket and any ambition. I jumped avidly on the opportunities. In the meantime, the small jobs nobody wanted presented themselves to help my shrinking budget.

Probably the most important induction to the American social stratification was a summer job in an after-school program in the Oakland Hills in California. It was a public school in the rather chic neighborhood of Montclair. The majority of the pupils were of Afro-American origin as were the headmaster and her main assistant. It was one of the rare instances when my poor language skills were a plus. In France, with the same level of proficiency, I would have never been considered for an educational venture. In Oakland, the fact that I did not speak like a White American was met with acceptance and sympathy. Little by little, I discovered the underlying racial tensions that were omnipresent among diverse social groups. I had no idea how deep these tensions went before sensing their presence in the workplace, particularly when a White young man joined our team. His presence brought some strain to a rather relaxed atmosphere. The fact that he was a bit lazy, treating this job as a short-term filler while waiting for a better employment, did not help his integration to the group and strengthened the underlying racial resentment.

The African American head teacher and her assistant were admirable educators and, in their private lives, tragic characters. When pupils were misbehaving, just a glance from one of them often sufficed to establish order in the ranks. The magic word "timeout" was hanging in the air as a threatened sanction for any disruptive nuttiness on the playground. There was also nostalgia for a mythical paradise of a far continent that these women had never known but longed for. We learned songs in Swahili or in its approximation and sang with children who represented quite an ethnic mix although the majority of them were African Americans. With time, the women disclosed bits of their private lives. They were separated or divorced. They referred to their former spouses as "druggies and losers." They ended up breaking their marital commitments at the point when the shared life stopped being bearable. The head teacher had fostered a boy who had not even been officially adopted but given up by his family for a better level of material care. This was, she told me, a frequent means of mutual support in African American communities, a residual communal feature of the primeval culture from which they had been severed by deportation and slavery.

Uprootedness was everywhere on that elementary- and middle-school campus. The children enrolled in the after-school program were brought up by working single parents who were in fact appreciative that their progeniture had a safe place until they came back from work. The atmosphere of the whole place emanated a longing for something that would rupture that impossibility of human closeness that we Europeans take for granted and occasionally find overbearing. Working in a cultural setting that was so remote from any of my previous experience was in fact exciting. I felt satisfied with a job that not many natives wanted or could do successfully. But, more importantly, it was a window to a deeper understanding of the American cultural and social reality. It was also an excellent induction into the university.

Grabbing one of the many options to complete my interrupted education, I enrolled in a state university where the tuition fees were nearly symbolic. It took some time to overcome the damage inflicted by the European educational system, whose goal was to level the student's self-confidence to the ground and show that the teacher was always right. The situation may have changed under American influence these days, but my European university experience dates from the 1970s and 1980s. Here in California, the students' self-confidence and lack of embarrassment at their ignorance were at first stunning and yet very refreshing altogether. One felt removed by a 100 light-years from the Polish evaluation: "Mister, you are simply an idiot." One could ask any question without incurring contemptuous remarks or gazes from the instructor. This atmosphere was no doubt conducive to scholastic success. It was always stimulating and encouraging when learning difficulties arose.

San Francisco State University was my first serious academic experience. To earn a BA in French, I needed to add two years of coursework to fulfill all the core residency requirements. At first it sounded frustrating, but once the classes began, I was delighted to be back in school; I was older than most of the fellow students, but there was a number of individuals like me who had returned to school after realizing that education was the greatest means of social mobility and that a state institution offered an inexpensive way of doing it. I liked all my classes, which I could choose from a rather large list of offerings. My favorite classes were philosophy, religious studies, and biology. The French classes for my major were too elementary, but soon I was allowed to take graduate courses that offered the missing challenge. Because of my major and the permission to take graduate courses, my university social life improved. Students preparing for an MA in French were of diverse ethnic backgrounds. It was these expats from diverse regions of the world who contributed to the collegial atmosphere of the campus. I spent long hours working there between my classes in the office of the Foreign Language Department. My interaction with peers who were for the most part not driven by sheer ambition but by the search for fellowship and the pursuit of knowledge for its own sake was the most valuable aspect of this experience.

The time for graduation came at light speed. The American system revived my enthusiasm for studies after it had been blown out by the European disciplinarian approach consisting of more punishment than reward. My professors encouraged me to apply to a graduate school. Getting used to the region of the Bay of San Francisco, I wanted to stay nearby and applied to the University of California at Berkeley for a program in Romance Languages and Literatures since I had added Spanish proficiency to my linguistic repertoire during my summer studies in Spain. I was accepted, and thus entered a new chapter of my life, that of an unintentional scholar. Berkeley represented an artificial oasis in the great Western desert. It is the most fascinating product of American civilization. In its unique way, it combines scholarly rigor with intellectual frivolity. For me, my years at UC Berkeley represented an antidote to the negative psychological impact of the European academic system, and, yet, the European heritage was always present in it. It was both an oasis where one could drink from the genuine sources of a solid academic tradition, and Baudrillard's anti-Ark, charged with human solitude and nonconformism, to anything established by sociopolitical conventions.

Todorov, who worked as a visiting professor in the United States, has lucidly analyzed the American university phenomenon. He writes, "In the United States, different in this from continental Europe, the university is, with few exceptions, outside the city, both geographically and ideologically…. We can never say enough about the effect this isolation, this institution of 'campuses,' our lay monasteries, has caused both in the city, by cutting it off from its thinking element, and among intellectuals by depriving them of the raw material for their thinking" (202, my translation).[2] According to Todorov, this wall between the intellectuals of the campus and the working masses in the city has resulted in a cultural bifurcation in which the two sides cannot find any common platform to fertilize each other intellectually. To the detriment of the university profession, those researchers working in the humanities have been able to freely indulge in focusing purely on methodology by adopting "French deconstruction" after uprooting it from its historical context and transplanting it onto the gated campus, disconnected from public life. Todorov pursues his charge by saying, "It is necessary, moreover, to be entirely cut off from public life and never to have left home, as these academics do, to take 'French' theories literally and believe that there is no difference between facts and interpretations, reason and beliefs, justice and interests" (203).

Such was the situation at Berkeley in the 1990s. Yet, the institution has had enough of a longstanding tradition of excellence to not collapse readily under the pressures of deconstruction. Soon, I learned from hearsay in Dwinelle Hall—the

[2] Tzvetan Todorov, *L'Homme dépaysé* [The Man out of His Homeland] (Paris: Editions du Seuil, 1996), 202.

building housing languages and literatures (except English)—who was who, who taught what, who was an ideological guru, and so forth. It appeared that there were still many outstanding scholars who taught serious courses without imposing their ideological views on students. Obviously, there were also those who represented a sort of new religion and whose courses were always filled with large groups of adherents forming an angry sect-like environment. With my acute sense of prudence, verging on paranoia, thanks to my upbringing in a totalitarian state, I always did my homework before choosing courses and almost entirely avoided courses overseen by priests or priestesses of decon-struction *à l'Américaine*. It was interesting to observe those professors who were demanding in a traditional way, who did not believe that there was nothing behind the text, who explained the historical context of the literary production, and who did not see or recognize or acknowledge how they too were compelled to pretend not to be unacquainted with the greatness of the "French" ideological imports. Here and there one heard a piece of jargon or a critique of literary canons for being authored by White males. The experience of doublethink from my Polish education was as handy here as it was in Poland. The shock that it was necessary to use it over here in this sanctuary of Free Speech passed very quickly. As always, real politics won. I realized that democracy had its limits and that it was a restless political reality making people angry and endlessly belligerent. Once I got over my naïve beliefs in the unrestricted freedom of democracy and learned the sneaky ways required to succeed in it, I thrived.

Yet, occasionally, a residual feeling of betrayal has beckoned to me, causing an ambiguous sensation toward the university's toleration of people like me who resisted its ideological fashions. Finkielkraut's more recent book *A la première personne* [*In the First Person*] brings some reassurance that my choice was the right one. He describes his own evolution as a student of literature (57–58). Early in his career, he adhered to the theories that focused on the text with no attention to its mimetic referentiality, as proposed by his early master Roland Barthes, who warned against "referential illusion," which he opposed to an "enchantment of the signifier." His encounter with Milan Kundera caused an ideological U-turn in Finkielkraut's critical perspective and brought him back to the appreciation of literature as "an investigation of the living world." Kundera, an exile from Czechoslovakia living in Paris, remained indifferent to structuralist or poststructuralist fashion; immunized by the cultural revolution of the Stalinist totalitarianism, he reaffirmed that the role of literature was to be engaged with reality within a historical perspective, that is to "advance, through new discoveries, on the inherited road" (Finkielkraut, 56, my translation).

While I soon adjusted to the academic and politico-intellectual idiosyncrasies of Berkeley, social life remained a challenge. Czesław Miłosz, a Polish American poet and a professor of Slavic languages at Berkeley and the recipient of the Nobel Prize in Literature in 1980, made an accurate observation regarding social life at Berkeley. In the introduction to his conversations with the Polish poet, Aleksander Wat (who was a visiting scholar at the university in the 1960s), published in the book entitled *My Century*, Miłosz comments, "As of now, more good people are to be encountered in America than in Europe. There is, however, a somewhat coarse and seemingly careless goodness because there is a low level of psychological intensity in human exchanges here, both of the good and the bad. If Wat, a typical Central European intellectual, had expected debate, deference, an attentive and devoted audience, he was sadly mistaken. He soon realized that no one had the time for long conversations here. That everyone was on [his or her] own."[3] Even though the conversations between Wat and Miłosz took place in the mid-1960s, in the 1990s the situation had probably intensified. The university had become more crowded and also more anonymous.

The PhD in Romance Languages and Literatures was a bit of a retro program with a great deal of freedom in choosing classes and a very small number of students because it required proficiency in three Romance languages and Latin. Gurus of deconstruction did not pay much attention to it because they preferred to focus on forming their own ideological disciples among those preparing a PhD in one language, who had no choice but taking their classes. In this context, I could slide relatively comfortably past the loud ideological debates on campus without ever engaging in them publicly. I acknowledge a certain dose of cynicism in my attitude that is not without connection to my conformism during the struggle against totalitarianism in Poland.

The disconnect between the world and the campus was certainly one of the sources of that hyperreality Baudrillard points out in his reflection on America. But being out of touch with reality is not due to the fact of an absence of ideologies as Baudrillard claims; "[America] is … suffering from the disappearance of ideologies that might contest its power and from the weakening of all the forces that previously oppose it" (115). On the contrary, I think, if we understand ideology as a forceful vision of reality as it ought to be rather than closely studying the forces at work in it, then America has become predominantly ideological

---

[3] Czesław Miłosz, Foreword to *My Century* by Aleksander Wat, trans. R. Lourie (New York: NYRB, 1980), xx–xxi.

but not youthfully idealistic as in its past when many countries looked up to it for inspiration particularly after the unfortunate divide between the West and the East of Europe. The ideologies that have become dominant in America have paralyzed its enthusiasm for serving the world with its democratic achievements. They have unleashed blind anger against the country's internal political entanglements, typical of a democratic system. Ideology has confused the existential failures one experiences in life with misfortunes caused by the others rejecting their own part of responsibility for unfulfilled aspirations.

Todorov's analysis also confirms this intuition. To illustrate this attitude, he provides an example of a person in Bulgaria who refused to trust the official weather broadcast because she believed it to be a lie, since all the other news on the communist radio station were usually "fake." So, when sunshine was announced, she always took an umbrella with her. This logic or its falsehood is to be found among many American intellectuals who, for example, used to claim not that Reagan was wrong because he had bad ideas but that the ideas were bad because they came from Reagan.

The tenure phenomenon on American campuses can unfortunately be a passport to self-indulgence, affording the recipient the freedom to lord it over his parcel of campus and voice his or her frustrations against a broad specter of power. The danger of this stance, according to Todorov, is that it may affect the whole aspiration to autonomy that should characterize any intellectual with moral integrity. He says, "[I]f an intellectual reacts automatically (for or against 'power'), if he calculates his words in view of the immediate objectives to be achieved, he renounces his very identity, which is to refuse the submission of his thought to anything else than the search for justice and truth" (1996, 204, my translation).

Thus, the tenured intellectual is awarded the potential to take revenge over the world for personal frustrations, inhibitions, and limits. In the humanities, the "French theories," cut off from their historical context, became the effective weapon with which to assault universality by reducing it to an oppressive grip of the powerful on the powerless, with no nuance. Such a vision of humanity seeks to erase progress in the institutional development we used to call civilization and suggest a return to the state of nature where force is the only valuable constituent of human development. Challenging this attitude, Todorov staunchly defends aspiration toward the universality of the human condition when he writes: "Finally, the possibility of consensus and the universalist aspiration are much closer to the democratic idea than the philosophies which see the world as prey to the irreducible war of races or nations, classes or sexes" (209, my translation).

While referring to the American intellectual landscape, I return to my own experience of the French educational system. I believe that universality ought to be treated with greater caution than the French system did when I was a student. A near-total imposition of the culturally interpretive framework on immigrants leads necessarily to resentment toward the host culture, which reminds many of the colonial past. Yet, I believe striving toward a consensus ought to be the only way if democracy wants to remain faithful to its principle of freedom and equality. Those who reject any idea of the universality of human experience and believe that the only truth is the truth imposed by the law of the most powerful are, in fact, advocating for an imposition of a totalitarian system. There is a middle way toward the truth by establishing the conditions that favor debate that can lead to a common accord through a state of discordant concord. The world, in its diversity, can work toward unity without suppressing the soul's nourishment by cutting it from its roots, as Simone Weil might have said. In his staunch defense of the French heritage, Finkielkraut should have taken into account the fact that it is not enough to defend this heritage but, above all, it is necessary to offer a scaffolding to cultural outsiders to help them access the French frame of mind. Without a proper pedagogical scaffolding, the climb is impossible; it will end up in a cultural split going deeper and deeper, as has been the case since the second half of the 20th century. The immigration cannot just be stopped; nor will a forceful assimilation ever be successful.

This is not to agree with those American intellectuals that the world is an arena of permanent wars between particular interests of diverse groups. An educational system ought to help natives as well as newcomers to find a cultural common ground. The objective of a humanistic education is to form not only open and tolerant minds but also critical ones. The critical sense ought to apply as to one's own heritage as well, so one can form a critical distance to one's own culture as well as to the foreign cultural import without a chauvinistic attitude of superiority. If critical thinking is deformed into blind opposition to anyone in power, as we have seen in the case of the Bulgarian lady's umbrella on a nice day, we adhere to the intolerant position and are on the path to a totalitarian, inflexible attitude that can only end in an interminable conflict.

Yet, it was my impression that American democracy, which never suffered any real danger from external totalitarianism, has found itself on the path to an internal implosion into an artificial set of proscriptions to limit its own cherished freedom. It is probably a sign of the deep spiritual crisis that American culture has been traversing since the war in Vietnam. The social liberation of the 1960s has brought down many previous taboos, leading to a broad freedom. Sexual liberation in particular has given women more autonomy in deciding their own future, both professional and societal. Compared to what I remember from the other side of the Iron Curtain, I can hardly sympathize with the tendency that wants to reverse implicitly those freedoms acquired by the Civil Rights Movement. Yet, this turn is real, and Todorov's impression helps articulate my own malaise regarding the current situation.

When Todorov returned for his last sojourn as visiting scholar at a U.S. university, he observed "the decline of certain democratic values and more particularly of the cardinal value of autonomy" (213). Todorov compares the position of the individual in the pre-revolutionary monarchy with the one in a modern democratic system. Under the *Ancien Régime*, the individual was subject to the royal power of divine right with a very limited autonomy. In democracy, individuals claim the right to be in charge of their own destiny; no government, even the one they helped to elect, has the right to interfere with the autonomy of the person. This right is applicable, nevertheless, to the political sphere and not the social space, which has to be shared with others. In the communist system, we wanted more autonomy in the political sense. To our surprise, the opposite trend has begun to develop in the United States. More and more people have never reached the emotional maturity with which to claim their autonomy in a democratic sense.

I can hardly refrain from a juxtaposition of this renunciation of autonomy with the situation in the Poland of the 1970s. In both cases, we see an absence of will to be the master of one's one fate. In the communist camp, it was the outcome of a progressive dulling of one's independent thinking; on one hand, by the propaganda; on the other, by coercive means: rewards and punishments. Individuals like me, once in a democratic system, found themselves completely lost in the reality where one had the freedom to decide about one's own future. It was as if one had to relearn how to walk without a walker or crutches. But one wonders why, in the country founded on the rejection of monarchy, and of any tyrannical tendency, additionally delimited by a strict observance of two presidential terms in office, are there citizens who surrender their autonomy to diverse clans or leaders who exercise a powerful ideological grip and do their thinking in their place?

One may suggest several explanations of this decline in the democratic value of autonomy. According to Todorov (214–217), the first reason for this state of affairs in American democracy is in part the lucrative status that victimhood has achieved in the United States. It is not to deny that many claims for compensations are valid. Nevertheless, the new ethos in the country is noticeable in the public media. We observe a replacement of the heroic ideal for the idealization of the oppressed. The heroic lone rangers in charge of their existence, defending their individual freedom through courage and resilience, have been substituted by permanent sufferers from evils inflicted from outside, accusing the world of their inability to cope with the vicissitudes of fate. One could provide many examples of this refusal to take at least part of the responsibility for personal failures or mishaps. Sometimes, one believes oneself to be the victim of inadequate rearing by one's parents; sometimes, one accuses the manufacturers of a machine when an accident happens. Another very troubling reality is that of sexuality, where the boundaries between what used to be known in the West as courtship, sexual harassment, and abuse need clearer delineation as the change of the ethos has affected the sphere of sexuality as well.

Todorov points out another element that contributes to the abandonment of autonomy. This political and cultural aspect radically separates the traditional European mentality from the Anglo-Saxon view of the problem. Currently, the issue has become much more sensitive in the American society than in 1996 when Todorov published his reflections. We notice a frantic need to belong to a group formed by either external racial characteristics or a common ethnic background or sexual preference. For the continental Europeans, the urge to belong to a group appears to be a denial of one's individuality and a betrayal of the democratic republican ideal of equality. Most of the democratic countries in Europe seek to neutralize political differences between various groups to form a homogeneous society where the individual rights of all are respected regardless of their skin color or other distinctive characteristics, and independent of their personal merit. In other words, the traditional republican model rejects biological or ethnic determinism of an individual. Of course, social practices have not always respected that ideal; nevertheless, the national regulatory efforts remain in place to uphold these principles. Current U.S. policies institutionalize difference by various bills encouraging separatism under the guise of valorizing diversity. This is found, for instance, in policies on employment and leadership positions. Hence, we witness various restless culture wars. As in the case of the cultural valorization of victimhood, the phenomenon of group belonging fosters a withdrawal from the public sphere of the nation into particularisms that induce emotional circularity, preventing subjects from deciding for themselves. Being part of a group forces one to relinquish one's autonomy for the sake of a collective power-seeking confrontation with other groups and to reject responsibility for one's own weaknesses, instead blaming the group that historically had more prominence and was indeed oppressive.

During my time as a student at Berkeley in the 1990s, all these tendencies were detectable. The town itself lived as a tributary to the great university. It attracted all those associated with protest as a permanent state of mind, both alumni of the university and migrants from other states where a rebellious spirit was less appreciated. It formed a community of rebels without cause, a collective that made itself feel good by adopting a collective frame of mind. Telegraph Avenue, with its display of nonconformist ways of being, exemplified the cultish overtones. Its street market, with stands full of Far Eastern goods, wrapped in a meditative mood induced by the smell of cannabis, hashish, or burning Himalayan incense, surrendered the explorer to its enchantments. The scene was hyperrealist in a Baudrillardian sense; only a rich capitalist society, that had no deep historical roots that allowed it to look at itself with a glimpse of irony, could take itself seriously and construct a simulacrum of the world with no referentiality to anything authentic.

Visitors from the Old Continent usually looked with disbelief and even envy at the freedom that merchants and other regulars of the Telegraph Avenue neighborhood exhibited. Speaking of exhibition, on one occasion, I was asked by one of my professors to show a prominent visitor from Oxford around the campus. Walking by Sproul Hall, a centrally located building housing the university administration, we ran into a spectacle at the door of the hall, a performance by "Explicit Players," a theatrical troupe that advocated public nudity. That day, the artists were performing in support of a rhetorics student called "the Naked Guy" who had been prevented by the campus police from attending classes in Adam's suit. My guest, a Rabelais scholar, and the author of the book *The Cornucopian Text*, found this encounter to be a sort of the cultural horn of plenty, symbolic of California.

Another time, I was showing a friend from Paris the alterity of Berkeley culture, and, while walking down Telegraph Avenue, we found ourselves in the middle of a pitched battle between a group of anarchists and the police. We managed to find shelter in a hospitable restaurant on the avenue. When we left the restaurant, we passed by several young people sitting on the sidewalk and bleeding from their noses. My friend found the experience thrilling, particularly the part when we were running holding hands not to be separated in the melee before we hid in the restaurant. It was like the scene from the American remake of Jean-Luc Godard's film *Breathless* with Richard Gere and Valérie Kaprisky. I realize that the artifice of the cultural climate of Berkeley was conducive to sparking associations with cinematographic imagery. Baudrillard captures this magic power in the following passage: "The American city seems to have stepped right out of the movies. To grasp its secret, you should not, then, begin with the city and move inwards to the screen; you should begin with the screen and move outwards to the city. It is there that cinema does not assume an exceptional form, but simply invests the streets and the entire town with a mythical atmosphere" (56).

During my time in the town, Berkeley permeated easiness and ephemerality in this kaleidoscopic movement of the sociopolitical events, with their imaginary stakes disconnected from the world beyond the boundaries of this ideologically enchanted island. At the end of the day, militants returned to their houses or shelters and tents (if they were homeless), to resume their struggle the next morning. Berkeley has always been "before the revolution," like the protagonists of the eponymous, highly lucid first feature by Bernardo Bertolucci.

The seemingly circus-like behavior found on the streets of Berkeley mirrored the hyperreality of the problems the residents of the beautiful town confronted. For a refugee who knew Poland before the fall of the Iron Curtain, the issue of public nudity was simply extravagant. While an explicit show was happening on Sproul Plaza, in Europe, the fratricidal Yugoslav war was destroying the historic town of Dubrovnik. There was the massacre of Srebrenica. A genocide was devastating the country of Rwanda. We were only a few years past the Tiananmen Square massacre. Here in Berkeley, sheltered from all that, with only a vague memory of the Vietnam War, people sharpened their revolutionary tendencies by agitating against the political status quo, rather like frequenting a fitness center with similar aspirations of being good to oneself.

The concepts of victimhood, identity, and difference are interrelated, as Todorov has suggested (221–231). Transferring responsibility on others for not fulfilling one's dreams has more weight if done by a group of like individuals with similar claims. When groups undertake their collective bargaining, they stress their difference to the detriment of the principle of inclusion. This struggle to preserve identity is all praiseworthy in theory, but it becomes problematic within a broader community composed of various groups staunchly defending their identitarian rights. How to incorporate the presence of many groups within one body politic?

The institutionalized support of difference by governmental agencies produces collateral effects that make it impossible to achieve unity of the body politic. According to Kołakowski, very few nations have achieved a balance in that respect. He has offered a valuable reflection on this neuralgic point of current democracies in the essay "Democracy Is Against Nature" (in *Niepewność epoki demokracji*, 169–177). His claim is that democracy must work against the state of nature. The world is naturally diverse. Nevertheless, human nature's penchants drive humanity toward divisions, and toward forming identitarian, exclusive collectivities of similar individuals. Yet, because the world is diverse, and pure national identity cannot be sustained in a democracy, unity is the solution for the peaceful survival of the body politic. And unity within diversity can be achieved by a conscious rational effort that seeks to level difference rather than rewarding its separatist assertions.

Kołakowski pursues his argument by presenting nation as the fruit of a natural development of human communities, arguing a nation thus has same the right to exist as any natural organism. However, human nature is inclined to violence and prefers using force to negotiation; in order to channel conflicts, culture has created a mechanism—democracy—to solve them without the use of force. Legislation and its proper functioning as the rule of law assure the order in the body politic, and most of the time the citizens who have elected their representatives to oversee the application of the law follow the rules to which they have consented. This balance between the natural drive for unrestricted freedom and a set of regulations to limit its destructive tendencies produces peace. History shows, however, that these periods of peace in the world are very fragile and prone to ruptures. The main danger for this equilibrium is an external threat, real or imaginary. When this type of threat is felt, self-preservation mechanisms become engaged. They might take the form of diverse nationalistic movements that attack democracy and try to subjugate it to the defense of the group that claims to have an exclusive right to represent the national interests. We find many examples of this break of stability today. Kołakowski mentions neo-Nazi movements in Germany, terrorist movements in Northern Ireland, Polish antisemitic graffiti instigated by "true Poles," and anti-Palestinian attitudes among some Israelis who are ready to commit terrorist acts to keep "Great Israel" intact.

How well does democracy function in the United States and how does it work toward maintaining the social equilibrium? Kołakowski defines democracy as a mechanism helping to reduce or assuage human conflicts through a system of rational rules that subdue overflowing passions and divert them toward a reasoned center. Applying this view of democracy to the U.S. context, we could say that America has unleashed these natural passions, these drives toward identitarian groupings, in the name of the aspect of freedom that in fact undermines democracy rather than serving it.

From Todorov's perspective, the factor distinguishing European democracies from the U.S. brand is American institutional support of differences rather than support for leveling them. The American political system fosters difference through a set of incentives such as quotas in hiring practices; such a solution to repair the social injustices of the past arrests the growth of civic virtue, making it even more difficult for a person to reach intellectual independence. It gives impetus to groups whose political claims jeopardize national unity and fracture the country's social fabric rather than healing its ancient wounds.

Todorov makes an important distinction (228) that the United States seems to have obliterated. It is a difference between civil society and the state and its administration. Civil society must strive to reach a maturity level in which the rules of democracy can be observed without coercion and constant intervention from the state. If civil society is not willing or ready to assume the rules the state proposes, we face the loss of democratic equilibrium. The state might be compelled to intervene in civil society and to regulate relationships within it. Nevertheless, too much interference in private lives by the state puts the country on the path toward totalitarianism. A unified civil society has its own set of cultural codes that operate spontaneously through internal negotiation. The democratic mechanism helps to establish the criteria that prevent from the violation of the codes of conduct. American society has blurred the distinction between the roles of civil society and of the government. By institutionalizing difference through state incentives, one crosses the boundary between the intimate and the public. Todorov believes that in the America of the 1990s there were no external factors to stimulate fears of a loss of national security. This reading of the situation could be extended to the 21st century. In a free democracy such as the United States, the implosion of the democratic system comes from the inside. By contrast, revolutionary groups emerging in totalitarian systems come to life as a consequence of the loss of autonomy at the hands of the totalitarian government. In the United States, the freest of all countries in the democratic system, groups form and willingly give up their autonomy. The individuals constituting these groups act as if they have been contaminated by a syndrome of victimhood. What European intellectuals such as Todorov or Baudrillard criticize is the broad cultural outlook on the world through the eyes of a victim. It is a violent world in which individuals or affinity groups blame each other or blame the leadership of the country for their existential *mal de vivre*. The Berkeley of the 1990s seemed to harbor conflict for the sake of remaining rebellious against the interior phantom of oppression that inhabited the souls of its residents. The revolutionary-like mood could be felt on the street of this university town and then in many classrooms. At the moment of drafting these pages I venture to claim that existential anger has contaminated many other parts of the country.

Experts blame the economy, the pandemic, ecology, the selfishness of the rich, and poor social policies. All that is true, but the question to ask is, why is it true? I believe it is worth returning to Weil's lucid remarks regarding the social ills of her time, which she traced down to the civilizational turn when the model of force became the only model for building institutions designed to conquer and uproot entire nations by force. Once social injustices reached the level at which they could no longer be tolerated, rebellions, insurrections, and world wars broke out. Yet rebels, if they won the battle, often could not but become oppressors themselves because the only thing they had experienced was force as the leaven for building their own culture, and they inevitably repeated the errors of their former oppressors. In the past, the ideologies that helped prepare rebellions against the social political status quo had recourse to Marxism as a standard leading them to the battlefield. As Kołakowski has suggested, Marxism-inspired revolutions concluded in even fiercer totalitarian regimes than the ones that had been brought down. History shows the failure of those ideological systems in bringing the promised happiness to people; it is enough to mention Stalin's Soviet Union, and various Asian countries where genocides went hand in hand with so-called social reforms.

Why has it not been possible to create a civilization that would fulfill the perennial expectations of humankind? Undoubtedly, progress has been achieved in sciences and in medicine. However, where is happiness? Where is what Aristotle calls eudaimonia? Why do people take up arms and blindly kill? Why do people drive trucks through peaceful crowds enjoying their leisure time? To kill in cold blood, one must be so unhappy that any traces of empathy must have been blocked in one's brain.

Simone Weil's reading of Homer's *Iliad* might shed some light on the contemporary *mal de vivre* in America as well in other parts of the democratic world. She ascribes the modern crisis to the rupture with the Hellenistic spirit that occurred in European culture, most importantly as a consequence of Roman imperialism. The title of her commentary *Iliad or the Poem of Force* suggests the main preoccupation of its author, which is the place force has occupied in the development of European culture. Weil claims that the Greeks understood the tragic predicament of the human condition, and Homer translates the universal tragic destiny of humanity. The tragedy of this destiny cannot be averted. There are no winners or losers in the Iliad. Both sides of the conflict are toys being tossed in the existential play of force. All sides are subject to its mechanics, and none can free themselves from its dominion. The difference consists only in the way in which one reacts to the permanent threat of being subjugated by force. There is always a temptation to hide in the self-deception induced by pride, humiliation, hatred, disdain, indifference, or the desire to ignore or forget (*Iliad*, 112). The only remedy that will allow one not to succumb to this temptation is grace and the practice of virtue. Weil discredits practically most of the epic poems posterior to the *Iliad* on the grounds that they have fallen into one of these temptations. In other words, they have missed the clarity or the lucidity of the Greeks' representation of the human condition by getting entangled in heroism induced by the blinding impact of force on reason. The fragility of goodness has been replaced by various deeds and triumphs.

According to Weil, the only texts that match the *Iliad* in its truth of expressing the Greek understanding of the human condition are the Gospels (113). This spirit appears in the representation of the Son of God incarnated in human flesh who shares willingly the experience of the human condition: He trembles in the face of suffering and death, and the abandonment by God the Father himself. There is no triumph in the accounts of the Passion of Christ: It is the naked truth of the human predicament—that truth lies in the fact of death itself. No humans can evade this destiny. And Weil uses the shorthand *malheur* [affliction] to refer to that tragic destiny. Those who think they can avert this finitude deceive themselves by hiding behind fantasy, falsehood, and illusion.[4]

Weil argues that Western culture has buried the tragic sense of human destiny somewhere in its evolution. She blames the Romans and the Hebrews for the disappearance of the awareness of the tragic sense and for giving in to the illusion deployed by force. The Romans despised everyone else but themselves; they substituted the gladiators' games for staging tragedies. The Hebrews saw themselves as a chosen nation and considered *malheur* as a sign of sin and, therefore, deserving of contempt (*Iliad*, 113). Christianity has become the heir of both trends through a progressive weakening of its Christological fragility for a triumphalist self-image, very much to the taste of its two ancestors, the Hebrews and the Romans.

[4.] On Weil's perspective on affliction and the need to live it to approach truth, see Lissa McCullough's "Truth and Affliction," in *The Religious Philosophy of Simone Weil* (London: I.B. Tauris, 2014), 20–34.

What would we see if we tried to perceive our own reality through the lenses inspired by Simone Weil's perspective? We would probably conclude that Weil's metaphysical *malheur* has suffered, so it seems, a plethora of travesties. Spirituality as a form of self-purification through the exercise of self-abnegation to reach the naked truth about oneself has given in to the appeal of force. The American context illustrates the current situation quite well given its postwar impact on the rest of world. Following Baudrillard's thought, the United States incarnates a "utopia achieved." Following Octavio Paz's take on America, he writes, "America was created in the hope of escaping history, of building a utopia sheltered from history, and that has in part succeeded, in that project, a project it is still pursuing today" (80). What is this utopia achieved, and how does it compare with other utopias? The most oppressive utopias that underpinned totalitarian states drove their all-encompassing ideologies on the track prepared by Marxism. They collapsed along with its symbol, the Iron Curtain. Until then, during the Cold War, America represented that different hope; its religiosity, its lack of any need for metaphysics, which was replaced by an acute sense of the immediate applicability of an idea to reality, and its love of the concrete, produced a culture that managed to dissimulate the universal ingredient of the human condition: *malheur*. In a very different way from the Marxist ideologies in the Soviet camp or in China, the refusal to question its self-confidence must eventually have led to a deep ideological crisis. It is possible, however, to see a parallel between these two systems that share the ambition to create a factitious reality that provides illusion for people to contemplate and thus feeds their fantasies about a better future. For the communist totalitarianism, it was a vision of a more equal world where, after the class struggle had ended, the thirst for progress would be quenched once for all. For America, this utopia achieved was in its materialistic scope; only the present and the immediate future count.

As an outsider to America, and yet someone who has lived most of his life here but resisted a full immersion, I keep wondering why there is so much protest, so much unhappiness, so much poverty in the materialist as well as spiritual sense. Everyone brought up in American culture who I have known in a relatively intimate fashion, to the degree it has been possible to know another person, emanated some degree of doom and gloom. What is gnawing at America, the utopia achieved, where the concrete human potential finds more fulfillment than in other parts of the world?

Two places with which I have become well-acquainted, and which I love to the extent it is possible to love something knowing that it will not be ever fully reciprocated, are Berkeley and Los Angeles. These two California landmarks are only superficially antagonistic. In popular wisdom, Berkeley stands for the capital of social progress, and Los Angeles, for a mix of outrageously wealthy conservatism with the liberal politics of Hollywood. In fact, these are two faces of the same coin. They are offspring of the same parents: capital and a-historicity. Baudrillard comments, "All other societies contain within them some heresy or other, some dissidence, some kind of suspicion of reality, a superstitious belief in a force of evil and the possible control of that force by magic, a belief in the power of appearances. Here, there is no dissidence, no suspicion" (85).

The comments apply to my experience of Berkeley. The university itself was founded in the 19th century, as one of the first public institutions without an explicit religious affiliation. Ever since, it has focused on sciences, theoretical and applied, and on the humanities: mainly art and literature. The school does not have a department of theology. The Graduate Theological Union (GTU) was founded in the 1960s to fill that gap though it has remained institutionally independent from the public university. Certainly, it has been a noble attempt to reintroduce religious preoccupations more closely to the secular campus. As a Berkeley student, I learned only later about the existence of the so-called Holy Hill, mostly through some fellow students who found it pleasant to use the GTU library as a quiet abode with no undergraduates around. Otherwise, there was rarely a reference to the holy neighbor. As I already described, Berkeley lived its life believing itself to be right regarding any subject or any political problem of the day. Somehow, Berkeley radicals proudly referred to themselves as the People's Republic of Berkeley, likely nodding to Maoist China and, in a good tradition of Maoist sympathizers, overlooked the collateral damage this ideology caused in the world. All in all, there was an anger, despite the overwhelming beauty of the natural setting and the charming architecture of the university building that Baudrillard would call simulacra. He was probably right in the sense that, besides the perennial enchanted setting, there was some void that a European would likely feel. It was the absence of roots in this brainy transplant from the old world.

If we admit that Weil is right when she sees in Greek culture the only true depiction of the universal human destiny as a fragile, delicate, and ultimately ephemeral stage blown out by death, then *malheur* must be constantly present in human consciousness. It appears though that none of the dominant political entities in the 20th century respected that truth. In Eastern Europe, totalitarianism deceived people by promising a distant but certain paradise while, in the meantime, it inflicted dire systemic misery on its society. The U.S. utopia achieved has fostered hard work and self-discipline in building the material welfare of the country. As the main outcome of that construction of universal happiness, we have an attractive simulacrum, a fantasy world that has banished the truth from its center and posited on reality an aura of mandatory optimism and self-appraisal. But *malheur*, that common feature of the human condition, could not be dissimulated; it needed to surface in some way. The ethos of solitary heroism epitomized by a lone ranger on his horse, by a businessman in his office, or by an astronaut conquering the space could not contain the existential *malheur*. All these heroic figures tried to harness force and drive it proudly toward success, but were stopped in their course by some mysterious blockage. The problem with the heroic attitude lies in the fact that it cannot halt the pursuit of the occasions for heroic acts; heroism builds on the use of force. A conquering hero causes casualties in his glorious assent and subjugates those who cannot withstand the course. This is a vague mirror of the American capitalist system. Culture misses a contemplative ingredient; it does not know the answer to the question, "Why am I doing it?"

Those who lost the course in this competitive society started rebelling and tearing down the heroic ethos. They felt used by the system and challenged it. Todorov has suggested that the appearance of the phenomenon of retrospective victim seeking reparation appeared in America when democracy reached its peak (229). It became clear that the judicial system had the power to secure the rehabilitation of the retrospective abuse. However, in a society founded on achievement driven by force, the former victims realized that by uniting in larger groups and pushing forward together, their legitimate demands would be met. The political system has supported the side of the victims, creating rules that protect them. The intelligentsia of American society no longer has the spiritual strength to seek the truth. Borrowing "French theories" and making them its own, it has helped the camps of former victims to arm themselves with ideological tools that give free rein to the construction of a simulacrum of truth based on mythological fantasies.

Currently the two sparring camps, the former oppressors and their victims, do like the two sparring camps in the *Iliad* where nobody is the winner in front of the terrible human destiny. The two American ideological camps have no insight about their share of existential misery: They opt for mutual accusations, believing that fighting is the only solution for their *malheur*. The ideology of success and competition does not offer any room for contemplation of the human condition. The utopia achieved has found another venue to fight for: reparation for retrospective wounds. Collective victimhood so far seems to be the most efficacious way of making the groups' voice heard. It is supported by the legal system in its supposed commitment to fairness.

The comfort of being part of a group requires maintenance. Its ideological engine is fueled by force expressed by anger toward the external world. The group's lack of a contemplative pause makes it impossible to have an introspective glance into its own ways of acting in the world. Weil offers a very lucid analysis of this phenomenon of forming factions that eventually lead to a political formation known as a party.[5] Their function is to secure power over other political entities. She writes, "Parties are public organisms, officially constituted in such a way as to kill in souls the sense of truth and justice" (26). It follows that groups, factions, or parties do not care for the common good but strive to impose the vision of the good that serves their particular interests. They intend "to kill the sense of truth," and, therefore, they transform the reality into a fantasy land to manipulate it at will. What would be a remedy for this state of affairs?

Weil and Kołakowski would agree that the only remedy for this situation would be a recourse to spiritual practices. Weil is adamant about the obstructive impact of factions on individual freedom. Human destiny is a spiritual one: the unconditional desire for the truth (*Note*, 38–39). A group imposes its ideology on all its members, thus obfuscating that "inner light of evidence," given to all so that they can use their faculty of discernment. They need to conform to the ideological frame of mind imposed by the party, its propaganda. Weil pursues her charge by considering the democracy developed after the French Revolution, founded on the parties' game where each partisan unit constitutes a little secular church armed with the threat of excommunication (39). There is something frivolous in the concept of a party that etymologically relates to the notion of an aristocratic entertainment in the Anglo-Saxon world (9). It diverts attention from the truth to the competition for power between diverse factions. Weil compares the social impact of parties to the abuse of narcotics and concludes that the state should forbid parties in the same way in which it forbids the public sale of narcotics. They intoxicate people, depriving them of lucidity and freedom, the basic needs of souls.

[5.] *Note sur la suppression générale des partis politiques* [Note on the General Suppression of Political Parties] (Paris: L'Herne, 2014).

Kołakowski's position is close to Weil's in his call for a higher moral authority in arbitrating the conflicts between various factions in society. Unlike Weil, who focuses on the divisive role of political parties, Kołakowski reflects on diverse ethnic groups within a state. The communists had put forward the promise that there would not be nations and nationalisms in the future. They would become anachronistic relics. Of course, recent history showed that none of these predictions materialized; instead, we observe a resurgence of various groups claiming the right to existence. There are two positions that propose different solutions to ethnic diversity within a state; one argues for an open society, the other for a closed one. Both positions find major difficulties when confronted with practical application in a body politic. An open society disregards the reality of the basic material needs of the population living on a territory. The influx of newcomers might cause imbalances in the social welfare of a democratic society. Proponents of an open society tend to ignore the material limitations related to territoriality and its needs and the fact that this would probably result in conflict. The closed society, on the other hand, runs a risk of transforming itself into a national totalitarianism. An extreme form of that totalitarianism might lead to ethnic cleansing. In this speech published in 2001, Kołakowski points out the rise of theocratic tendencies in different parts of the world. Many seek the support of a religious affiliation to strengthen their sense of identity. It is perhaps, Kołakowski suggests, the break of secular ideologies that died out that contributes to the recourse to religion as an ally in overcoming the identity void. But religion allied with a political party loses the role religion ought to have: the teacher of our humanity.

Todorov and Finkielkraut do foresee religious influence in arbitrating conflicts but suggest the solution be based in dialog between the factions involved in a dispute. Dialog as an essence of the democratic functioning of a community must be politically supported. The absence of dialogue signifies a deviation toward totalitarianism. Todorov and Kołakowski had known the impact of the absence of dialogue in their personal lives. They both experienced exile, and once the communist system collapsed, they expressed the desire to see the implementation of democratic values in their countries of origin. Nevertheless, the process of reconstruction has been much slower than was hoped by all who celebrated the collapse without bloodshed of the Soviet camp in 1989. The following chapter reflects on the political and social meanderings that occurred in Poland after the collapse of the Soviet Empire.

CHAPTER 6

New Poland: A Steep Curve Toward Democracy

There is nothing so noble or a message so full of kindness that, at the devil's whisper, it cannot be turned into a murder weapon. The work of the devil invariably consists in poisoning our good sides with hatred and using it in the interests of hell, and we succumb to its temptations over and over again.
(Leszek Kołakowski, "This Devil's Freedom. Meditations on Evil," 156)

Thirteen years after I arrived in Paris in 1981, a few months before the imposition of martial law in Poland, I was free to visit Poland. I went along with a liberal, progressive, American friend, anticipating finding in Poland some of the clichés about the Slavic soul and temperament. We faced disappointment. Poland was confronted with a drastic economic plan known as a "Shock Therapy," which was supposed to bring the country in an accelerated fashion onto the path to the capitalist system. Instead of the joy of reconstruction, we found an overwhelming gloom caused by the brutal transformation. My American friend was surprised by the lack of courtesy, by the roughness of the surroundings, by the tiredness of the people walking on the streets. Indeed, the street crowds reminded me irresistibly of the images from the film adaptation of Emile Zola's novel *Germinal*. I tried to hide the fact that I was a resident of a Western country, not to attract the hostility of the crowd passing by. It was not easy as I was in the company of my English-speaking friend.

Many Poles showed signs of hopelessness in face of the new system that required intellectual agility and adaptability. The younger generation was up to it, but the older Poles, whose conscience had been formed in the totalitarian system, did not have those qualities. The new system not only broke the chains of the communist system but also revealed the deeply rooted scars of the past regime. These scars are the legacy of "homo sovieticus," the perverse psychological product of the system that had been informing people's behavior in the way of subservience and passivity. It was easy to feel it looking at bitter faces during that first visit. When asked about the post office, the answer would be something like this, "in the past there were many more offices around here; the new government has closed half of them down." The same was said about a small grocery store: "They open a supermarket at the outskirts of the town; our store could not survive the competition." At that time, I realized that my American friend could not understand any of it. Maybe the post office did not have enough customers to remain open? To a Westerner, Poland showed itself as a gloomy, bitter, inhospitable place, and there was no use trying to explain anything; the cultural distance was simply too deep.

To make us feel more at home, we discovered a splendid McDonald's situated in the ancient building just by the medieval gate known as Brama Florianska [Florianska Gate]. It was located not very far from the popular café Jama Michalikowa (lit. Michalik's Den), which was founded at the turn of the century by a certain Jan Michalik. It has kept the atmosphere of the *fin des siècle* by keeping the old décor. In my childhood, my mother used to bring me there for ice cream at the conclusion of our occasional trips to Kraków. My childhood memory of the past suddenly became contaminated by the present, my present as an American resident, and my past as a child of Southern Poland; to add to the confusion, I was in the presence of a friend who had no connection to these memories, to their meanings, or to the meaning of the McDonald's next door. As a liberal, my friend saw in McDonald's a symbol of the American imperialism, and Polish naiveté, or a lack of understanding of the complexity of American culture from Poles, to whom the American psyche was inaccessible.

The Polish fascination with America goes back to the War of Independence, which can be compared to the participation of Polish heroes like Kosciuszko, and Pulaski in the fight for Polish Independence. Poles who don't know much about the internal politics and social conflicts of America want to see a power-ful America that remains the world policeman, with its military and economic domination over Russia. This explains the honorable location of McDonald's in Kraków. McDonalds represented what used to be the privilege of the Pevex stores' customers during the communist era. In the 1990s, McDonald's symbol-ized an opening of the doors to the Western material abundance; an average Pole could taste Western delicacies freely without having to pay for them in dollars bought on the black market. This preference for foreign products would remain unchanged for a long time.

Visiting my family on that trip brought some relief because they were doing better than the average Poles, thanks to the survival skills the generation who lived through World War II learned during that time and knew how to apply those skills to various circumstances. During the communist era, they knew how to use the black market and how, who, and when to bribe to maintain a decent quality of life. They pushed their children to study medicine, dentistry, or engineering, the professions sought out in any political system. When communism collapsed, the new generation did not have major problems adapting to the free market. Looking at the new Poland, I realized how fortunate I was to have left just in time. With my degree in the humanities, I would have been part of the Germinal-like crowd: tired, bitter, and disillusioned.

My first visit back prompted a question about the new identity of the people among whom I grew up but with whom I could no longer fully identify. How has Polish identity been evolving in the transition from the totalitarian system to the free market? What has been at stake in this transition? How deeply has the Catholic Polish society been involved in this transition? After that first visit in the early 1990s, my trips to Poland have been almost yearly. Yet, short stays could not provide sufficient matter for understanding where Poland was going culturally and ideologically.

Invaluable insights have come from intellectuals who have analyzed this transition period and offered critical evaluations of the burgeoning Polish democracy. Two figures that stand out as most integral commentators on Polish reality are Leszek Kołakowski and Józef Tischner, both already mentioned in the chapter on America. For both of them, the political transition in Poland unveiled a complex legacy of totalitarianism in this process of shedding off the skin of the old system. In one of his books, *Nieszczęsny dar wolności* [The Unfortunate Gift of Freedom], Tischner scrupulously exposes the contradictions within post-communist Polish society. His concern is the legacy of "homo sovieticus." It is a Sisyphean undertaking to eliminate the dormant specter of the psychological deformations of totalitarianism. It reappears under avatars resembling various expressions of freedom. When those who desired freedom all their life found themselves confronted with it, and they felt at loss in the expanse of the possibilities it offered.

The case of the Catholic Church is particularly interesting. This powerful political entity has assisted the Polish population in surviving many invasions and occupations throughout history: the war with the Teutonic Knights in the Middle Ages; the Swedish "Deluge" in the 17th century; the period of the partitions of Poland in the 18th and 19th centuries; the German occupation; and the Stalinist and post-Stalinist persecutions of the 20th century. The Church in Poland was seen as a champion of the right to the national independence movement for centuries. This militant characteristic of the Church, particularly in its confrontation with the communist government, strengthened its political and social position in the country. The Church of Poland did not share the Church's persecutions and demise in the other countries of the Communist Bloc. This fact did not go unnoticed in the Vatican circles that led to the election of the Polish Pope, John Paul II, in 1978. It is remarkable that the Catholic Church in Poland shone with a particular glow in times of the national dangers of which Polish history constitutes a crimson-dominated mosaic.

To my surprise, during my visits, I could feel a growing anticlericalism among the population. On the Church's side, one could sense a mood of triumphalism, mitigated by the new challenges of a free-market society. Tischner, a philosopher and a clergyman, offers a highly lucid analysis of this critical transition period for the people of Poland. The country has entered a new phase in its history. After a few centuries of dreaming about freedom, political freedom has become the new reality. I can immediately relate to the challenge by recalling my experience of finding myself in Paris and being frightened to use that new freedom. I recall my own paralysis and the initial impossibility of acting in an environment that required initiative, creativity, and a revision of personal biases. It took years of rejection and blame of the new freedom before I was able to stand on my feet again and walk without gripping a support for fear of falling apart. It was only that inner mysterious light that has never gone out allowed me to overcome the crisis.

How has the entire nation been coping with this avalanche of freedom expressed by new laws, new ways of doing business, new attitudes toward education, and new fashions from the West? Obviously, it must initially have been a profound setback for the march of freedom. The working class of the totalitarianist period resembled the exploited coal mining workers of the 19th century, neglected both physically and spiritually. The radical economic reforms, and the sudden disappearance of the obvious enemy in the communist system, unsettled the population. The Church had a unique chance to enter the dialogue with the new social reality that freedom offered, but, according to Tischner, this chance has been lost by the triumphalist attitude that followed winning the battle under the standard of the Polish Pope, John Paul II.

As Tischner points out, this was a shortsighted perspective on the Church's part. It was blinded by the initial gain in power and influence and failed to realize that the generation born after the fall of the Iron Curtain would not have the same affective relationship to the pontificate of John Paul II. The new generation would be immersed in all capitalism has to offer: materialism and entertainment. The young Poles would receive from their parents a superficial, reverential account of the Polish Pope's legacy that didn't apply to their own experience. Moreover, the freedom of contact with the West would certainly provide the younger generation with echoes of critical views on the pope, widely broadcast in the West.

The new freedom was to find itself on trial well before it started growing some roots in Polish society. Blame became the main characteristic of Polish public life. Freedom has been blamed for abortion, for pornography, and for the return of the former communists to power. All that is attributed to freedom whose impact, little by little, supplanted in gravity the danger from the former abuse of power.

Tischner points out this great paradox of the human relationship to freedom. People fight for freedom, not knowing precisely what it entails. Quoting Dostoyevsky's tale of the Great Inquisitor, Tischner reminds us that people, given freedom, will trade it for slavery and material goods rather than live in the state of perpetual discernment freedom requires. People tirelessly seek a master to whom to give up their gift of freedom. History shows us this in the German nation's disastrous flirtation with Hitler. The Soviet Revolution ended up with an equally cruel dictatorship.

It is therefore not surprising that political freedom, having been awaited for generations, has become the greatest problem for the new Poland. The Church had known well how to deal with external invasions by providing moral support for resistance to the foreign rule. In the new context, it had a new enemy, the free market to whose arrival the Church had contributed. In the past, its canon of commandments and prescriptions represented an antidote to the oppressive regulations of the totalitarian system, and for that reason, the Church's teachings were accepted even though they were hardly observed in full. This has changed since the free-market economy imposed itself on people's life with its new enticing propaganda; advertising replaced the old political propaganda. Alas, the Church responded to it by reinforcing its prescriptive attitude, blaming Western influence for spreading its anticlericalism on the Polish cultural landscape. Rather than looking to the new needs of the people provoked by the reality of materialism, the Church—charged with its evangelizing agenda and ignoring the devil's enticing call for more power and more possessions, the great temptations of capitalism—failed to enter into dialogue with the new, liberal, perspective. It appeared as if the Polish Church needed a new enemy to thrive again, but the enemy was hidden, entangled in people's aspirations and in the Church's defensive attitude.

How to serve people in the new capitalist reality is the question that remains unanswered. The context seems to be more reminiscent of a political battle than of an organic growth of the people and their Church, who walked together through difficult times of totalitarianism, reached the destination, and realized that the common life is no longer possible. The remedy for this state of affairs might be the urgent realization by the Church that the promises of materialism that make people forget about spiritual needs are the new enemy. An inner transformation is required in the whole culture. And the Church needs to pay careful attention if it doesn't want to become part of the same worldly realm only by reverting to the tactics of the secular world.

Simone Weil's warning about the Catholic Church's temptation to become something of a militant political party might be of greatest inspiration in the question of how to exit the current cul-de-sac. Blame is probably the chief characteristic of the secularized democracies in the world. If the Polish Church insists on maintaining its political power, it cannot win the battle with the forces of materialism. Instead, it should look to its original strengths that provided it with its spiritual appeal.

Tischner has suggested in the chapter of his book entitled "Christianity in the Post-Communist Void" (79–91) that the religious landscape in the free Poland has been dominated by a Manichean anxiety about the prevalent existence of evil in the world. The experience of evil at the hands of the political power epitomized by the gulag, the symbol of political persecutions, and the permanence of propaganda distorting the truth have left a legacy of mistrust about the possibility of overcoming evil in a free post-communist society. Tischner refers to this phenomenon using Paul Ricoeur's concept of "hermeneutics of suspicion." According to this attitude, evil has not disappeared from the post-communist landscape; it has adopted different tactics for damaging society. Therefore, post-communist individuals see everywhere the potentiality of evil. People have not really changed; they just wear different masks. Mistrust leads to intolerance toward the other. The new democratically elected government is seen as a travesty of legitimacy. The resurgence of the specter of the past dictatorship inhabits the Polish national psyche again.

How should religion address to this spiritually recessional period? The Catholic Church seems to be feverishly reviving those Manichean fears and trying to capitalize on them by acquiescing in attitudes from the old times when the Church was the main opposition to the communist evil. The all-encompassing apprehension of human beings fosters the image of God as a harsh vengeful judge, and salvation is contingent upon the total submission to God's absolutist rule. This is not very different from the oppressive impact the communist party had when it dispensed its judgment on the citizens, followed by rewards or punishment accordingly. There is not much room for the God of the Gospels, the incarnate God, who feels for the sinful woman, God of the Good Samaritan helping the distressed. It is the God of force who rides his chariot like the one depicted by William Blake in his series of representations of the divine.

The question that the Church in Poland must face is the about image of the God in the free world. There will be a progressive erosion of the image of the fearful judge as the process of secularization advances. God the intransigent judge will lose his appeal in a society that will plunge eventually into an infatuation with the pursuit of material well-being. In a secularized society, God might choose to die leaving it in an abysm of desolation with no other purpose than waiting for its own death. The Church must return to the source that the Gospels represent and revise its role in the new reality. Poland still has the Catholic capital of past resistance to communism but needs to invest it differently. It cannot deploy trench warfare because the enemy is no longer the same; it attacks from inside. The trenches on the other side of the front are empty. It cannot wage war on the corpse of the Polish People's Republic. The time has come to reevaluate what is the new role of the Church in a democratic reality.

Poland must go beyond reactionary behavior toward criticisms and stop reverting to attitudes that were necessary during the fight for independence. The country needs to examine its recent past in the light of the new system of which it has become an integral part. It cannot treat the freedom that comes with democracy as a new enemy. Democratic reality requires self-control in daily life. The concept of civic virtue had been erased in the totalitarian system. Civic virtue was then associated with subservience to the ruling political party, expressed in most extreme cases by spying on others and denunciation. Democracy calls for the free assistance of citizens in serving the common good and maintaining order. When the chains of totalitarianism fell off, the autonomy of action did not follow immediately. Walking without chains turned out to be even more difficult. This is all understandable for someone who lived at that time but who was also immersed in Western freedom and had major difficulties adapting. Yet, it is time to embrace new directions for Poland's religious and secular culture.

In more recent visits to Poland, I was surprised by the rhetorical excess of the press. Serious periodicals of diverse political spectra use imagery and verbal expressions that in the West one finds only on the grocery stores' shelves in *The National Enquirer*, *Star*, or *Daily Mail*. I didn't even dare to open any of these publications as I didn't want to be burned by the hateful fever that emanates from their pages. TV news programs in general project an image of mediocrity and a lack of taste reminiscent of communist times.

With the fall of the Iron Curtain, an ephemeral hope for the New Poland has arisen. Alas, as the quote from Kołakowski suggests, Poland, the dedicated daughter of the Church who has entrusted her fate to the Queen of Poland, the Virgin Mary venerated in the Shrine of Czestochowa, has remained blinded by her desire to reconnect with her imaginary special place under the Sun, forgetting the dangers of falling into the devil's snare of nationalism. Adherence to the European Union has helped economic integration to a certain degree, but it has also left Poland stagnating in the status of a poorer partner, who eventually became difficult, using all its rights as a member to curtail the political influence of the European Union.

CHAPTER 7

Spirituality: The True Source of Rootedness

Midway along the journey of our life
I woke to find myself in a dark wood,
for I had wandered off from the straight path.
(Dante, *Inferno* [trans. M. Musa])

Life was good, the weather splendid, funky stores with various health supple-ments enhanced the mood, and a cucumber lotion softened and hydrated the skin. And all was almost perfect in this "utopia achieved" except for dreams that kept coming back, evoking a dark labyrinth with no exit. They were no longer like those Parisian dreams with the haunted streets of Kraków blocking the escape gate to the free world. It was a limitless expanse of an exotic forest with a dense growth of luxuriant vegetation through which I was trying to carve a path, in vain. I woke up on my futon to realize that I was in the happy place of Berkeley and that I needed not to worry about finding a way out. Why were these dreams recurring with such intensity?

I was about the age of Dante at the time of the composition of his Inferno. The preparation for my qualifying exams had plunged me more intensely into the malcontent bent of my immigrant personality. I very badly needed a guide. I envied Dante who had Virgil as a rational guru in his crossing of Hell. Of course, Berkeley was nothing like Hell, but it was the space where hell and heaven met to obliterate any sense of guilt, any sense of inhibition I had been impregnated with in my upbringing. And from that perspective, I saw in it a form of *danse macabre* beckoning to the revelers to join the party.

A Pole living in the United States faces the multilayered stigma dating back to the time of massive immigration from Europe at the turn of the century. Often illiterate, with rough manners of a rural living, this group has set the image of a backward, dirty, and ultimately stupid population that became prey to a collection of ridiculous (occasionally quite funny) jokes. Yet in my encounters with Americans, I experienced a clash between that image and my own identity of a Pole born during the communist era, benefiting from a rather good public education, and a careful upbringing by the parents who belonged to the intelligentsia, a rather poor but educated social category. I was a vegetarian for some years during my time in Berkeley, not a kielbasa eater or vodka drinker to fit the stereotype still in vogue in the 21st century. In ecclesiastical circles, I appeared as a curiosity to be tested about my allegiance to the legacy of John Paul II whose rather tough conservative grip on the Church particularly displeased the generation of Baby Boomers who have been awaiting the second coming of the summer of love in vain.

My imperfect but staunch Catholic faith should have come to me in rescue from entering the imagery of that prelude to the end of the world. It did not at first. While my past and present contacts with the Polish Church raised reservations about an enthusiastic and full adhesion to her ways, my encounter with the middle-class American Catholic Church resulted in distrust as well. Whereas the Polish Church did not pay much attention to the individual welfare of the parishioners, the American Church did quite the opposite. I had the impression that the divine had been substituted for the divinization of the congregation. The atmosphere could be summarized by the chant, "All Are Welcome," which goes, "Let us build a house / Where love can dwell / And all can safely live / A place where / Saints and children tell / How hearts learn to forgive." In my mind I translated this chant as "Let us build a house where anything goes."

The church's atmosphere was in sharp contrast to the nearby campus inhabited by competition and strife. Perhaps, from the contextualized point of view, in America as the utopia was achieved, this church and her chant made sense. For an outsider with a totalitarian past, wrapped in layers of cynicism, this came across as a supreme instance of self-indulgence. During one Holy Week, I felt the need to go to confession to expiate for my doubts and dislikes of what I saw in the church. The encounter with a priest in the open space of the church happened to be superficial and devoid of meaning. In my Jansenist inclination, I expected for penance something in the line of flagellation; instead, a smiling parish volunteer gave me a white carnation. This symbol of the renewed purity of my soul did not convince me; instead, it deterred me completely from further attendance of that church. I switched to the Hispanic worship in another part of the town. Seeing faces of the tired immigrants, their sense of awe, and the absence of intellectual preciousness brought me back to the atmosphere of Poland but without its clerical authoritarianism. Spanish masses represented a sort of lifeline with the Catholic tradition in a landscape that was clearly unfamiliar.

Yet Spanish masses did not take away my dreams of aimless wanderings. For a long time, I avoided any political engagement in the controversies of American academia. Yet my immersion in the paradise/hell of Berkeley was reaching its conclusion. I looked at the academic job ads; most of them were beyond the scope of my political disengagement. I had escaped submission to totalitarianism and was not up to suffering another form of submission to something I did not believe to be true. The facility of my American peers in pretending to adhere to a school of thought that entailed the indispensable support of the influential faculty was admirable. It reflected the process of how the utopia achieved has been sustained. It occurred to me, not without surprise, that the underlying characteristic of institutional power operated similarly everywhere by resorting to coercion grounded in the potentiality of force. Of course, there were superficial differences, but the deep mechanism was comparable. One scholar of influence attracted a larger following of students who showed outer signs of reverence by sitting in the first row in a lecture hall and by nodding regularly in reaction to some statements that they could replicate in their own discourses, thus marking their discipleship.

Despite my admiration for certain professors, I was not disciple material. There was in me a mistrust of authority, probably induced by my experience of the school system in Poland that meant I associated the school master with the ideological oversight of the political party. While in Poland, the faculty's allegiance (to a different degree) to the authorities was for the most part an involuntary servitude; on the U.S. campus, this servitude was voluntary. In many cases, this form of discipleship was motivated genuinely by a quest for the truth. Nevertheless, in many cases, the voluntary servitude was the fruit of the desire for a comfortable academic career for which endorsement by a renowned professor was a condition.

Who was I in this space with no hell and no paradise, but the "utopia achieved" with its own laws promoting self-realization? The Polish hereditary call for transcendence began to inhibit any temptation to indulge in what Berkeley offered. The greatest temptation was to try to assimilate, to fit into the culture that would help discard the unhappy past so that, for once, I would be good to myself. That threshold appeared to be impossible to cross. I could try explaining it by my psychological deformation due to the totalitarian system combined with the guilt of a Catholic immigrant aware of being luckier than most of the people of my generation who remained in the country. But that was superficial.

There must have been something more than a psychological block. "Midway along the journey" of my life, I was lost in the dark forest of my soul. To get out of the dark forest, I needed to cross a different threshold than the one leading to complacency about the culture I was immersed in at that point.

In my journey through the dark forest, I encountered a few bright shining light posts. It was a time of writing my PhD thesis, the topic of which was inspired by a professor from France who offered a seminar on 17th-century French literature with its connections to Italian and Spanish letters. The experience of writing had a spiritual dimension as I realize now, having acquired some "professional" credentials in what is referred to as spiritual exercises. It was the experience of "The Dark Night of the Soul," to evoke the famous poem of the Carmelite monk John of the Cross, which was probably composed during his confinement at the hands of the rival Dominican order in the 16th century on suspicion of heresy. I felt a breach in my being that was opening to an external influence of some sort that carried with it a breath of unshakable optimism.

Tedious work on a first major writing project became progressively more rewarding as my familiarity with the three authors grew. The 16th-century Italian poet, playwright, and literary theorist, Torquato Tasso, felt immediately close to my heart. It was his personality described by his biographers that exercised an irresistible appeal. There was an inadaptability to the social political context Tasso and I had in common. He was a misfit in the Ferrara court of the Este family. He tried to fit the system the best he could but always felt or was made feel inadequate. He imposed on himself rigorous rules of poetics whose standards he could not meet in his own work, so he believed. He accused himself of an excessive inclination to *ozio*, idleness that infiltrated his writing sneakily but surely in forms of *diletto*, pleasurable melodramatic sequences compromising his outer commitment to the prescriptive rational severity proclaimed in his own treatise on poetics.

Studying Tasso, I realized my own entanglements within the hedonistic charm of Berkeley and my resistance to it were caused by some inner persuasion of a higher calling rather than indulging into what the pleasure-seeking Berkeley had in its hyperrealist bounty. I was a misfit to comfort and stability. And yet, there was a side of me that had a penchant for easy, lazy, and uncommitted ways of being, which California encouraged. Also, there was a voice of reprimand, as if coming from my father, denouncing my idleness, and my traits of character inherited from my mother's side of the family. Was my father's intuition really prophetic when he saw in me a tendency toward indiscipline and disorder? Yes and no, my answer would be. I grew obsessively disciplined with time but utterly disorderly regarding space. My lodgings, be it in Paris or Berkeley, were characteristically untidy and cluttered, but my sense of time has remained perfect. Obsessive punctuality was my father's trait as well. That connection to time, I realize, has been a manifestation of my defenses against a disintegration of my identity. I could not control the space around me, I have lost my literal roots, and the notion of native soil on which to stand has become irrelevant. Nevertheless, the abstract notion of time has made it possible to travel through time freely populating memories. Memories fill the present to preserve what has been lost in a physical spatial sense.

In my monk's cell, while drafting my dissertation, I indulged in imaginary visits to Santa Anna hospice where Tasso was confined because of his violent outbursts of madness. I wanted to consult with him about my own struggles with my failure to adhere to what fate has given me by anchoring me in the place that could have become for me an existential "tabula rasa," making it possible to start a new a comfortable existence when the past would not matter anymore. Yet, there was an overpowering sense of duty to stay connected with my roots through imagination by actualizing key events of the past. But imagination in the soft climate of Berkeley made them appear less traumatic than they actually were.

In his treatises on poetics, Tasso fought against certain types of poetic practices most prominently represented by his contemporary rival Ludovico Arioso in his popular epic poem *Orlando Furioso*. The poem ostentatiously violates the rules of verisimilitude propagated by those theorists who claim that epic poetry should not implement any elements contradicting the laws of nature. For instance, there are flying horses, and magic rings making people disappear, in Ariosto's poems. However, the unsophisticated readership seeks to be entertained and they have no misgivings about the presence of those elements in the poem.

Reading and writing about those debates and controversies in Renaissance Italy against the backdrop of the folkloric streets of Berkeley, I felt they resonated in me with a particular intensity. I readily identified with Tasso's position about the need for rigor and discipline in the representation of what matters or should matter to the world. A certain dose of didacticism was needed to instruct the *vulgar* about what is good, what is decent, and what is frivolous. The Berkeley town was *ariostista* in its cornucopia of flamboyant happenings on its streets. There were no flying horses, but one was not very far off from finding a sorcerer on a street stand trying to sell a magic crystal or some potion that would make one fly as high as the Moon. It was a carnivalesque body with pretentions to establish a self-centered commune that ostensibly ignored the world's plight outside Berkeley's walls. Tasso's ideological commitment to the truth, sometimes at the expense of a corrective representation of reality, was ultimately reassuring to an immigrant from the outermost place on Earth in relation to this current abode of plenty.

By tracing Tasso's impact on narrative theory, with guidance from the course taught by the professor from Paris, I was led to the neo-Aristotelian revival of poetics in France. The French Academy appeared to be extensively influenced by Tasso's treatises. The Parisian intellectuals of the 17th century were assembled by Richelieu in the institution whose mission was to preserve the French language and its letters from the vulgar lawlessness of popular culture. I remember not liking 17th-century French literature at my first contact with it. I found it pompous and could not relate to its rigorous aspirations to rise above the taste of the common people. All these ancient queens or kings sounded wooden in their tirades, and their commitment to higher realities such as common good, virtue, and honor, all projected a passé fashion. The Alexandrine verse did not help me to focus on the message. A few years in Berkeley, the antipode of French rational restraint, and the proper introduction through coursework to how to read this literature in the context of its production, caused a full U-turn in my reception of it. It prompted a new appreciation of its high ideals regarding the role of literature, language, and art in the life of a political entity.

Simone Weil would not have been proud of my choice of Pierre Corneille as my main author but would have approved of Tasso because of his conflicted attitude toward his theoretical stance on poetry and his own practice of it. Tasso believed that he betrayed his own prescriptivist poetics by giving prominent space to human weakness and failure to sustain virtuous conduct in the face of sensuous temptations. Corneille on the other hand pushed the application of the neo-Aristotelian rules to an extreme. His play *Horace*, followed by his controversial *Le Cid*, was fiercely criticized by some members of the French Academy for its indulgence regarding the rules for the composition of tragedy. Chastised, Corneille waited a few years, and showed in *Horace* that he could do it. The protagonist of the play, the Roman soldier Horace, is so committed to the state that he does not even back away from killing his own sister, who chooses allegiance to the anti-Roman camp of the Curiati, to which her husband belongs. Simone Weil saw glorification of the Roman military virtue as an example of the extent to which the Christian civilization separated itself from the message of the Gospels. The play stages the role of force in the construction of the powerful state by eliminating any dissent to its overpowering march to subdue individuality. Weil qualifies the play *Horace* as follows, "Corneille was right to dedicate his *Horace* to Richelieu, and to do so in terms whose baseness provides a suitable accompaniment to the almost delirious pride which permeates this tragedy. Such baseness and such pride are inseparable: we see that well enough in Germany today. Corneille himself is an excellent example of the sort of asphyxia which seizes Christian morality when it comes in contact with the Roman spirit" (136).

But reading the play in the freedom-loving Berkeley felt good. A type like Horace could make a difference in confronting its citizens' wanderings and surrendering them to some realistic purpose that would curb the city's individualism. Even though Horace could be seen as (or, in fact, was judged as such by some commentators) a prototype of a fascist in his uncritical submission to the state's all-encompassing rule, for me, it represented a force that could possibly serve the body politic by imposing on it self-discipline against individualism and self-indulgence. The city of Berkeley with its nearly constant protestations against American imperialism is indeed a product of a capitalist system that allows a marginal social entity to flourish as a proof of the freedom of expression that political and economic liberalism guarantees. Complaints about imperialism from people who live comfortably off it are like a teenage rebellion against parents who keep on providing in spite of ingratitude. There has never been a Berkeley-like city in North Korea, or even Russia, where such subcultures are more closely monitored if not suppressed completely. An example of that monitoring is the fairly recent action by President Putin against what was seen as a cultural performance crossing the limit of tolerance. The five members of Pussy Riot, a Russian feminist protest punk rock group, staged a performance inside Moscow's Cathedral of Christ the Savior. At least two of them ended up in jail labeled as "foreign agents." In Berkeley, it took a long time to find a pretext to prohibit the behavior of the Naked Guy. The reason for the ban had to be something with sexual harassment of the departmental secretaries whose offices' windows were exposed to the usual path on which this individual liked to parade. Even though in both cases we see an absurd pretext for the ban of the behavior in question, the democratic system requires a certain degree of sophistry before proceeding to action against the undesired conduct. The totalitarian regime needs none of that. Blaming foreign agency is an old totalitarian trick that was used to send thousands to the gulag.

In an attempt to escape reality, I grew in sympathy with Tasso's vulnerability and let my imagination wonder about a figure of Horace who might bring some orderliness to the revolutionary Berkeley. Ultimately, I decided to disengage from those concerns and allocate my preoccupations elsewhere. I transferred my focus to the sphere beyond the politics. I keep acknowledging with a dose of guilty emotion that I have always shied away from politics, which I have perceived to be necessarily contaminated with dishonesty induced by the thirst for power. I experienced an outburst of aversion when I began to inquire about my prospects of getting an academic position. The job hunt was necessarily impacted by politics, and my chances of getting an interview were practically nil, with no prior knowledge of political influences on the job market. I watched my peers closely, who had the amazing skill of packaging their statement of purpose politically, addressing particular institutions with job openings. I too attended workshops that offered practical advice on how to craft a job application in order to attract the attention of a prestigious institution. Yet, my roots in a non-capitalist reality, in the land of mistrust, prevented me from compromising the legacy of my parents in their resistance to the lure of collaborating with the system they despised. Rather than jumping on an opportunity, by surrendering to its ideological design, I opted to remain free in my appreciation of authors for their affinities with my own persuasions.

A dark night of the soul descended on me with an unusual intensity during this final stage of drafting my dissertation, my experience of the demands of the job market, and my personal, nearly obsessive grip on values from a different world. My Catholicism, preserved by the life-giving connection to the Hispanic community, acted the way it had acted in the rebellious Poland; it pointed to a transcendent reality that made the quarrels of the day or the egocentric religious performances irrelevant. From the lectures of the professor from Paris, I learned about the impact of Jesuit schooling in the 17th-century theater in France. I found out that Tasso and above all Corneille were intellectual products of Jesuit educations. Suddenly, I realized the unexpected connection between these facts and my three-year work experience in Paris in the 1980s at the Jesuit school, Saint Louis de Gonzague. There was clearly something mysterious about this coincidence, whose discovery brought a sense of inner joy that overrode my gloom about my inadaptability to the progressive Berkeley.

This was a transnational connection that unexpectedly valorized my time in France. I had not just wasted nearly a decade over there on different jobs of which the position at the Jesuit school was the culmination. How was it possible that I found myself again under the umbrella of Jesuit intellectual impact here in the neo-Pagan Berkeley? I tried somehow to understand this impact, but in vain; the sources I used for my dissertation essentially stressed the pedagogical aspect of that influence without mentioning a spiritual element. Yet, the underlying spiritual element drove that pedagogical approach, whose ultimate goal was to form pupils capable of resorting to spirituality in their political or broader decision-making. Commentators limit their analytical focus to the use of theater as a didactic tool for presenting ethical choices. They also emphasize the role of theater in promoting political ideas; it is particularly useful for serving the absolutist agenda of the monarchy. It is certainly true that Corneille's theater is particularly representative of this tendency when his characters debate possible ethical choices, and the one who supports the state's interests identified with the common good usually wins. Yet, I certainly agree with Simone Weil when she dismisses Corneille's theater as a fruit of the corruption of Christianity by the Roman spirit. It is true that Corneille's optimism is the optimism of a warrior who blindly focuses his energy on the battles ahead. The Christian spiritual element becomes a casualty of the will to power. Corneille's poetics divert considerably from Tasso, who struggles to find the linearity of the spirit of conquest in his poem *Gerusalemme liberata* and fails to subdue the fragility of the human predicament to heroic indifference à la Corneille.

Attracted more to Tasso than to Corneille, I pursued my intellectual adventure, seeking to evade the reality of my rather comfortable life as a graduate student. Clearly immune to what I strongly believed to be a path of falsehood, an academic career at the expense of inner freedom, I kept walking through the dark forest, persuaded that there would be a clearing at the end of the road. And indeed, there was a lamppost at the end of the crossing of the luxuriant forest of Berkeley inhabited by carnivalesque creatures enacting what they believed to be serious political ideas powdered with sensuous aroma of eternal youth—but what they missed was the true sense of the possibility of eternal life. Berkeley revelers wanted eternity here below and acted as if this desire for eternity could be fulfilled by their own doing.

At this point of my introspective writing, I realize how important my cultural roots were for my resistance to embracing the happy environment of the California town. Simone Weil's insights again come in handy for this self-analysis. Stressing the difficulty in defining what it means to be rooted, Weil attempts to define it as a "real, active and natural participation in the life of a community" (*The Need*, 41). "Natural" means here to be a fruit of the circumstances in which one was born and brought up. These circumstances include the geographical place, the birth conditions, profession, and social surroundings. In my case, there has been an existential precipice that separated my ethnic roots from my host culture. Weil points out the importance of intercultural exchanges, but such exchange ought to operate as "a stimulant intensifying its own particular way of life" (41). For me, the fact of being transplanted to the utopia achieved stimulated my desire to become someone more than an immigrant. I genuinely wanted to dissolve my otherness in this melting pot, but there came an issue of "digestion," to invoke Weil's metaphor. American cultural impulses acted like a catalyst without entering my soul as Weil would want it—"[The roots] should draw nourishment from outside contributions only after having digested them." I realize now that I suffered from cultural indigestion, and there was no remedy around to alleviate the discomfort caused by the fact my roots could not grow deep enough to satisfy my longing for a new identity.

What was the reason for resistance? Perhaps, the simple fact that no one wants to be brutally uprooted and transplanted to a foreign soil. Weil cautions, we remember from my prologue, "Whoever is uprooted himself uproots others. Whoever is rooted doesn't uproot others" (45). Perhaps, I found myself in a culture that lives off its own uprootedness and multiplies various simulacra of the real for the lack of the original piece. But because of this absence of the primal reference, it needs to innovate and produce more and more to compensate for the referential vacuum. The absence of historical roots translates itself into an absence of the contemplative skill that only rootedness makes possible. By contemplative skill I mean the capacity to stop one's run and reflect on the past: ones' geographical place, birth conditions, profession, and social surroundings. But when the past contains an uncomfortable truth, the easiest way to address the issue is to forget about it altogether. America was founded by the uprooted peoples who came to this country having been deprived of their life-giving connection to the context in which they were born and raised. They came to this continent with the hope of recreating the original context, but obviously all they could achieve was to create a simulacrum of the old country. The uprooted people who came to America in turn uprooted the indigenous populations by progressively conquering their lands with a messianic enthusiasm accurately labeled as "Manifest Destiny." The ideology of Manifest Destiny was at the antipode of what Weil calls "real, active and natural participation in the life of a community." It equaled the ideology of uprootedness disseminating cultural desertification on the conquered territories.

So, here in the desert of the American West, immersed in a proliferation of concepts, objects, and easy ways of living, I exited the dark forest only to enter a plain desert of the soul. A vast desert from which one could escape only with the help of God or Mammon. I had seen Mammon too many times already and had not succumbed to his temptations. While traversing that desert I could not opt for the easier solution, which would be to take the path of compromise and comfort. That would involve reversing course and swimming with the flow of the political currents flattering those who, like those in power from whom I had fled half a century before, would assist me in securing a decent job that would allow me to subsist for the rest of my life with a feeling of security.

The interior desert intensified the thirst for something otherworldly. I skimmed the pages of my dissertation; the sections on Jesuit education retained my attention. I grabbed from the shelf Marc Fumaroli's book *Heroes and Orators* and reread the sections on Jesuit theater. It was at the time of the emerging Internet. I typed the word "Jesuit," and, among many entries, I saw Jesuit School of Theology at Berkeley. I could hardly believe this coincidence. It looked as if I had made a full circle from the Jesuit school in Paris to this School of Theology in Berkeley. The coincidence certainly defied any rationalization. I thought it could have been a desert mirage from which I wanted to escape or maybe an external intervention of fate or providence. I was not able to tell the difference at that time, and it did not matter. I looked more closely at the site and found a contact address, so I set out to explore the possibility of entering this Catholic religious order. Two years later, my fate was sealed: I applied and was accepted. One thing about this adventure is sure: I have touched something that went straight to the depths of my entire being beyond the distraction of the simulacra of reality propagated by my current surroundings.

My new focus on spiritual matters has brought me back to my religious roots that had been hibernating, buried by the circumstances of immigration. It was an awakening of the inner treasure I kept buried in my soul. It was truly liberating to reconnect with something that was foundational of my identity. Yet, the baggage of 20 years since my departure from Poland could not be erased; my return to an active form of faith had to absorb what had happened between my innocent embrace of faith as a child and the mature man's experience of having seen the two sides of the equation: the struggling Eastern European Bloc and the materialistically opulent West. This renewed faith has expanded my horizons beyond the surface of nationalism, party membership, economic concerns, and affinity groups. I have gained the sense that these transient preoccupations ought to be treated not only with due consideration but also with the necessary distance so that they do not become idols or substitutes for the ultimate reality that encompasses all of them and prevents each of them from overshadowing the truth of human existence.

"What is the truth?" Pilate asks Jesus Christ during his trial after not under-standing of Jesus's enigmatic answer to the question of whether he was the King of the Jews, "You say rightly that I am a king ... I have come into the world, that I should bear witness to the truth" (John 18:37–38). Weil's stance on the Gospels and Greek stoicism comes immediately to mind. She exhorts, "It is from the Stoic conception of *amor fati*, love of the order of the world, regarded by them as the supreme virtue, is derived. The order of the world is to be loved because it is pure obedience to God. ... everything, without any exception, joys, and sorrows alike, ought to be welcomed with the same inward attitude of love and thankfulness. ... Those men who disregard the true good disobey God in the sense that they don't obey as a thinking creature ought to do, with the consent of the mind" (*The Need*, 275–276).

Religious life, imperfect as it can be, forces one to accept that sense of Prov-idence that Weil's equates with "the regulating principle of the world" (272). The Spiritual Exercises drafted by Ignatius of Loyola, the founder of the Jesuits, represent a manual of spirituality by which a "pilgrim" can attain a level of indifference to the changing order of things in the universe. It is a physical and psychological initiation into acceptance of the world's beauty and working toward shielding that beauty from the violence inflicted by pride and self-rigorousness. Ignatius of Loyola and Weil would probably agree with the statement that we ought to love the world as it is, even when this world is punctuated by outbursts of unspeakable evil, caused, as Weil suggests, by disobedience to the order of the world. Since humanity has been dosed with "the desire for the supernatural light," it can err in fulfilling that desire. That errancy is the cause of evil. The remedy for evil is goodness attained by love. Therefore, compassion and love ought to be the guiding principles for maintaining or recovering the order of universe. Love is actually a commandment, not a spontaneous infatuation with a particular attractive manifestation of reality. Ignatius calls it "attachment." Attachments are the outcomes of human desire gone wrong, that is, of breaking away from the order of the world as the divine Providence has conceived it. Accepting the constraints imposed by the religious order, I have been able to conform more to the order of the world: I have revived the connection to my roots.

CHAPTER 8

The World's Totalitarian Temptation

> The unhappy people of the European continent are in need of greatness
> even more than of bread, and there are only two sorts of greatness: true greatness,
> which is of spiritual order, and the old, old lie of world conquest. Conquest is an
> *ersatz* greatness.
>
> (Weil, *The Need for Roots*, 93)

I am writing the final chapter while the latest resurgence of the spirit of conquest and empire is breaking through the apparent harmony the European nations have enjoyed until very recently. It is astonishing to read this quote at the time of the Russian invasion of Ukraine in 2022. The media incessantly shows hundreds of thousands of refugees fleeing the areas affected by the invasion. My imagination has been impregnated with media images of destruction and chaos during the Russian attacks on the Ukrainian cites. I just had a dream similar to my recurring dreams in Paris about the inescapable labyrinth of the streets in Kraków. I was hiding under the table from the bullets hitting the apartment I was in. Waking up, I thought of all those individuals who are having dreams not impregnated by images from the media but from the reality they had witnessed.

World cultures are showing again that they cannot establish a political reality where dialogue and compromise allow the flourishing of their populations. Weil's concept of existential *malheur*, the tragic sense of human life, is camouflaged by the proliferation of a kaleidoscope of commercial temptations sponsored by the owners of technological gadgetry. The easy fabrication of virtual images exceeds the apocalyptic prognostics of thinkers such as Baudrillard who feared the spill of America's hyperreality into the world. Now, the whole Earth can be wrapped with imagery sponsored by groups that project their commercially subdued vision of the universe. Relatedly, Simone Weil was scandalized when the illustrated periodical *Marie Claire* could be found in French villages. It corrupted the local sense of belonging to the *terroir*, shattering its organic continuity. It ultimately led to uprootedness of the population from what had been sustaining them for centuries.

In our time, this danger of uprootedness has multiplied by the nth power. The imagery of luxury life in richer countries causes waves of immigration, creating millions of uprooted people who become a new proletariat, deprived of their identity, and economically abused. The mass media cannot stop diffusing their commercial, often sexually charged messages to their audiences. Yahoo, for example, on its news page gives the accounts of the atrocities committed in Ukraine next to the news about a celebrity posing in a sheer dress. The burning problems of the world are blurred with marginal events blown out of proportion in their societal importance. Yet, they appeal to the emotional sphere of the psyche of the masses, dissipating any sense of moral judgment in differentiating the good from the evil. The global outreach of the Internet amplifies the power of the masses' uncritical passionate impact on reality. The real becomes a matter of molding the facts forcefully to satisfy the pursuit of an ever-changing illusory world. The real undergoes the process of transformation to become hyperreality, a virtual utopia governed by netizens with their expectations of instantaneous satisfaction of their desires. If those desires are deferred, one can expect street riots. Justice that requires time and discernment struggles to preserve its freedom from the passionate pressures of the crowd. It is as if the world were not able to reach the age of maturity but remains in the stage of infancy where desire ought to be satisfied right away and, if not, there will be screaming and stomping.

Individuals like me, formed in the totalitarian system, dream of a world where transparency and justice reign in the public sphere. In my political innocence, preserved for too long by the Iron Curtain, I hoped to find a world where truth and only truth mattered. It was an outcome of growing up in a political culture that was free enough to allow us to think that the ideological foundation of the system was wrong. But knowing that ideologically all political discourse consisted mostly of lies did not foster a critical thinking or a deeper existential reflection on what it means to live a good life. My Catholic upbringing gave me a sense of good and evil but did so in a rather mechanical fashion without helping me to understand the subtleties of how good and evil operate in this world. Brought up by parents who rejected the political system altogether, I made projections based on literature, films, and periodicals I discovered in the French library in my university town. I fed my imagination with this imagery as the French peasants probably did when they found an issue of *Marie Claire* in their village, which eventually inspired them to leave the countryside to the city and live like the people on the pages of this illustrated magazine. In Kraków, *Paris Match* was my *Marie Claire*. When the border of Poland opened a few months before the martial law, I went to my imaginary paradise: France.

There it took some years to shed the skin of a *homo sovieticus* unable to live in a free-market reality where one struggles to find a place in the system where the government will not tell anyone what his or her place in the social fabric is. As for the truth, that was to be even more complex. I had thought that the Westerners would all think like my parents did, that there will be a clear separation between the truth and falsehood. I did not expect to find any sympathies toward the Soviet government or communism itself. In the 1980s in France, the Communist Party was still alive and well. I found myself tossed between the right, which was sympathetic to me for having fled the oppressive regime that was meant to die, and the left, which used my presence as an occasion to show that the socialism as it was in Central Europe needed urgent reforms to survive. The collapse of my truth brought from Poland and my inability to function in the system plunged me into a deep existential crisis that lasted a few years until I started appreciating freedom along with all the personal challenges it carried with it.

Nevertheless, the sense of uprootedness was not going away. I grew up within an uprooted reality of postwar Poland. The lives of my parents had been shattered by the German invasion. Even though I lived in a small locality, my parents were not from there originally, and that mattered particularly for my father who never reconciled with the destruction of Warsaw or with the new Polish army that pledged its allegiance to the Soviet command. Having absorbed uprootedness from my family hearth, I carried it away to France. After a few years of living and working in France, I could eventually pass for a French native. But I was acutely aware that I was an alien to the culture I had thought one day would be completely mine. The prophets of assimilation have it wrong that one can assimilate to a new culture and grow new roots in it. It did not happen to me in France, and I sympathize with all who share the sense of uprootedness in a place to which fate has brought them, regardless how amicable it might be.

When America unexpectedly became my new home, I expected to ground myself eventually given its reputation of acceptance and tolerance of diversity. It was all true about acceptance but also radically untrue regarding the possibility of overcoming the sense of otherness. Whereas the French manifested different political attitudes than I had been accustomed to in Poland, socially they were quite similar to the Polish people. There was a desire for human warmth and fellowship. Americans were quite a different species. Although I must amend my comment that my social interaction has been limited to the university context. I have had a limited exposure to various ethnic enclaves America prides itself to have. However, my reflection concerns primary the college-educated social class and university employees as well as sectors of the Catholic Church.

Compared with Poland or France, America differs in its relationship to reality. Whereas in Europe uprootedness is certainly present, in the United States the phenomenon of uprootedness takes a radically different dimension. The country's foundation is uprootedness, that is, a sterile land acquired by conquest and populated largely by the uprooted peoples who were forced to leave their homelands because of famine or political persecutions. They united in a utopian dream of building a reality without bad memories. America is a final stop for all who flee the reality of the human condition. Those "refugees," internal or external, find here an artificial oasis that quenches their thirst for oblivion. The universal existential *malheur* drowns in the soothing waters of that oasis whose most spectacular incarnation is Disneyland. The concept of the amusement park is to leave existential worries behind and enter the world of childlike fantasy, unrooted in the land of struggle for survival.

In certain ways, the American utopianism is a distant cousin of the French revolutionary idealism that had tried to erase the past and build a new culture on a tabula rasa by offering a new calendar; or more recently, it is reminiscent of those cultural revolutions in some communist countries. Unlike communist countries, America has been able to construct a superficial culture of *fun*, avoiding the gloom and terror of her communist cousins.

Whereas the communist cousin has been operating on the repression of desire by forcing a sense of collectivist responsibility, its American relative has sought to produce means of immediate gratification. Uprooted imagination, purged from historically grounded conventions and seconded by sentimentality, has produced a culture whose appeal was soon to overpower the depressed realities of the communist camp.

Paradoxically, these two apparently exclusive conceptions of reality have one common strand in their ideological DNA. They share a prophetic vision of the world molded according to their conceptions of it. Communists have banished God as an external intrusion threatening to sanction their behavior in the pursuit of the fulfillment of their "visionary" plan for humanity. Neoliberal capitalists have domesticated God to serve their manifest destiny in spreading the system around the world. In one of his more recent books, *The Totalitarian Experience*,

2011, Todorov offers a synthesis of the perception of the totalitarian system he had known from experience and whose residues have plagued societies not only in the former communist camp but also in the countries where capitalism has developed without any major obstacles from powerful anti-capitalist ideologies. Todorov suggests that totalitarian communism shares with religions the postulate of the role of Providence. It supposedly draws on the laws of history. It rejects the subjection of its theory to examination and forces on it the label of "scientific." There is obviously nothing scientific about it, as Weil, Kołakowski, and here Todorov (10) have shown. It is much closer to the order of prophecy than anything to do with the laws of history, which have always evaded doctrinarian visions. This postulate of historical ineluctability legitimizes violence and war in advancement toward the disappearance of all differences among human groups. Only then would humanity be able to live without conflict, having abolished property and given to the state the administration of all instruments of production. This postulate promotes a secular messianism or utopianism, very much parallel to some religious teachings, with the exception that the paradise is to be attained here below through revolution or war rather than in a distant afterlife.

According to Todorov, the secular version of messianism does not stop at this idealistic proposition for a new design of the world. It elaborates strategies that aim to concretize that design by using force and violence. If it were necessary to eliminate an entire category of people who might oppose it, this act would be fully justified by the higher ideological calling. This strategy was used by the two most lethal totalitarian regimes: Hitler's Germany and Stalin's Russia. The ethnic cleansing of Jews and Slavic peoples by Hitler and the extermination by hunger of Ukrainian peasantry and confinement of opponents in gulags by Stalin were preferred methods for building societies according to the ideological designs of those leaders. By recurring to those strategies of terror, the goal of totalitarian messianism was to first transform the political institutions and subsequently to create new human beings who would eventually obey and defend the system by spying and denunciation.

In the concluding chapter of his book, Todorov draws intriguing parallels between communism and ultra-liberalism. These ideologies have, according to Todorov, a common ancestry in their assumption that human social existence depends on economy and, therefore, a "scientific" knowledge of the underlying economic laws is necessary for social progress. They differ in their approaches to social welfare. Ultra-liberalism calls for suppression of all obstacles to the individual will in the development of the free market; the claim is that individual competition should be freed from any constraints imposed by the state's inter-vention. Communism proscribes individualism, imposing authority from the collective will of the state. This inhibition of the individual will was meant to produce a homogeneous, just society in opposition to the unregulated state of economic affairs in a liberal system.

Both systems have failed to bring about a social equilibrium. Both thrive on uprootedness of the major part of society by forcing its subjects either into fierce competition, leaving along the way many economic casualties of their prosperity gospel, or by frustrating any original will and condemning it to a vegetative state of mediocre collectivism. Both systems operate on their messianic assumptions that the truth is on their side and that the only way to build social progress is to either politically impose the "scientific" laws of history on the entire population or to clear any limitations to the "natural" and, therefore, "scientifically attested" laws of economy that regulate human social existence.

After the collapse of the official communist system, the Western world did not know what to think about the new ideological landscape. Todorov argues that in America, there is a distance from the communist experience in Europe, and an ambiguous attitude toward the Cuban revolution, which had many good social motives, even though it was supported by the Soviet regime, whose intentions were certainly more militarily strategic than fraternally altruistic given Cuba's proximity to the United States. All in all, the Cuban challenge to the United States has left an aura of sympathy toward communism. It is worth adding the frantic experience of McCarthyism, messianic in its core, that has left a dose of sympathetic ambiguity about the anti-communist attitudes of liberal Americans.

Having lived most of my life in the "free" West and become more and more disturbed by the world political situation, I ask myself if the "free" West has a chance to free itself from spells of secular messianism diffused by various propaganda channels. The answer that imposes itself is clearly "no." The incur-able conviction that there is something good about the totalitarian providential design of Marxist ideology has permeated well-meaning progressive groups in Western society. In Western Europe where communist parties were allowed to operate legally, their sympathies toward their counterparts in the East could hardly be dismissed. As we remember from my encounter with the French left, from whom actually I greatly benefited when starting my life on the other side of the Iron Curtain, they admitted some mistakes in the communist countries, but overall, they would not change their conviction about the necessary course of the political advancement toward building a new, better, class-free society.

In America where the Communist Party has been prohibited, there has been a "progressive" consciousness with the underlying belief that, in fact, the communist system might have been right at least partially. The history of communism is less known in this country, and the current influence of still existent communist propaganda makes it difficult to present the real impact of the communist regimes on common people's lives. Moreover, the overwhelming ignorance of history and geography in American society makes American culture a fertile ground for all sorts of deformations of reality and factuality. The major American universities have not been spared from this disease. As in the Western Europe of the 1950s and the 1960s when intellectuals overlooked the existence of gulags in the Soviet Union to praise its social reforms toward social justice and equality, American intellectuals, cuddled by the luxury of campus life isolated from the reality of the blue-collar existence, have absorbed cynically or naively the "Kool-Aid" coming from residual Marxism. The revisionist movements that recently swept the major American cities might be traced back to those progressive sympathies germinating on U.S. campuses. The current climate of revisionism is reminiscent of the 1950s in Poland, when young militants from the uprooted blue-collar and rural social classes tried to dictate to professors what and how to teach under the threat of disruption and denunciation of any insubordination to the political authorities.

Contrasting secular messianism with the religious one, Todorov points out that most traditional monotheistic religions offer their adherents the choice to reject providential design at the expense of divine retribution. This is true for mainstream Catholicism. Communist messianism denies any degree of freedom of choice; it reduces its providential design to this world by borrowing from religion its transcendent absolutist perspective of salvation and confining it to the limits of its earthly influence. Violence, terror, and spying are the means of bringing salvation to all at the price of their freedom. The outcome of this indoctrination is *homo sovieticus*.

Confronted with illusory ideologies, first encountered in France and later in America, and inspired by some Marxist reassurance of the historical necessity, I made many trips to Poland once I established myself in the United States. I witnessed the same struggle I had undergone in my process of adapting to the new democratic system. Within the span of 30 years, Polish society has been trying to find itself in the new reality in which the future was no longer clearly delineated by a messianic vision of a class-free society. In the initial phase of reconquered freedom, Poles breathed the fresh air, still filled with an idealistic notion of freedom. Soon they were to learn about the price of freedom they did not expect to pay. Idealized capitalism began to send bills for its plethora of material goods that filled the shelves of the stores, which were empty during the communist era. The government opted for the radical method of bringing Poland to the free market. The population was shocked by the impossibility to satisfy the appetites created by bold advertising. Voices of nostalgia for the communist past with no room for entrepreneurship began to rise.

Liberal economic policies soon caused great social disparity in wealth. Rapid technological advancements deepened the gap between those who could learn and adapt to new ways of working and those who could not update their professional skills. This gap paralleled the generational gap. Despite the atmosphere of discontentment, the Polish governments of the first decade after the independence from the Soviet domination managed to reconstruct the economy well enough to make it possible for Poland to become a member of the European Union.

One of the casualties of that period was intellectual life. During the communist period, Polish culture benefited from the state's subsidies even though artists and writers had to wrestle with censorship. Some followed the path paved by the official propaganda, but many walked a fine line between the threat of being "canceled" and the need to remain in peace with their conscience. Some of the most prominent went into exile. In the new independent Poland, the freedom from censorship produced a proliferation of mediocre imitations of Western commercial publications, films, and shows, often challenging good taste and sexual decorum. The Catholic Church initially benefited from the collapse of the oppressive system and recovered some of the possessions lost to the communist state. Most importantly, the Church managed to impose religious education in public schools, a step that was to have an ambivalent impact on Polish society. From the account I heard in Poland, the Catholic religion classes were frequently staffed with either priests or lay catechists who had poor teaching preparation, making those classes dull and irrelevant. Many students did not have any good experience in those classes, leaving their religious education with a sense of burden rather than life-affirming inspiration.

Paradoxically, as I recall, my religion classes were also dull and uninspired, but the attendance of catechism was seen by the majority of Poles as a political statement against the government's hostility to Catholicism during my school years. It was not required. The instruction took place in the presbytery, and the two priests who taught us were both terrible teachers. But my sensitivity to the subject matter was present, and I learned eagerly from the textbooks at my disposal. Comparing those two realities, I appreciate Józef Tischner's analysis of the Polish Church in his book, *The Unfortunate Gift of Freedom*, in which he challenges the Polish Church in its embrace of a nationalist theocratic stance in Poland's emerging democracy. Kołakowski also expresses his critical attitude toward the ways the new Polish democracy has been approaching these challenges. In many of the essays and papers collected in the book *The Uncertainty of the Age of Democracy*, he exposes the difficulty and fears of Polish society in its attempt to balance democratically the drive toward the preservation of nationhood and the acceptance of the cosmopolitan influences to which democracy must remain open. In this conflict of interests, democracy is the tool to channel, weaken, or even resolve conflicts without recourse to violence (169). We could add to it the useful distinction Weil makes about patriotism and nationalism (*The Need*, 97–98). Patriotism is the love of one's roots grown on a given territory without claiming an exclusive right to it. It is the individual's rooted link to the past with an outlook to the future. Nationalism, on the other hand, calls for the sponsorship of the state and promotes the ideology of the superiority of one's own ethnicity and cultural heritage; it is contaminated by the drive to conquer. Kołakowski warns against the unbalance between patriotic self-respect and the drive toward national supremacy usually leading to despotism in the country and to war on the international arena. Actually, in the article "Democracy Is Against Nature"[1] from 1999, he urges to look for warning signs about the possibility of war in the foreseeable future if they are not detected soon enough (176). As it happens, we are in the middle of the war in Ukraine at the time of drafting these pages.

The role of the Church should be, therefore, that of a mediator between the nationalist passion and the social order that makes it possible for the nation to remain open to external influences without giving up its identity. These conflicts of interest must be solved through dialogue and persuasion. As it is now, so it seems from Tischner's analysis, Kołakowski's cautioning, and the accounts I have heard in Poland, the Church has opted for supporting the nationalist camp flirting with the idea of a prophetic role in Poland as a Christ of Nations.[2] According to this messianic vision, during the past two centuries, Poland suffered partitions, occupations, and foreign dominations, but resurrected from this dismemberment

---

[1.] "Demokracja jest przeciwna naturze" [Democracy Is against Nature], in *Niepewność epoki demokracji* (Kraków: Znak, 2014), 169–177.

[2.] On the notion of "The Christ of Nations" in Polish culture, see Timothy A. Byrnes, "The Catholic Church and Poland's Return to Europe," *East European Quarterly* 30 (1996): 433–448.

like Christ did, and now its role is to help resurrect Christianity in the country and outside. In the current context, the Church needs to learn how to work within the democratic reality that still remains external to the national psyche. The specter of authoritarianism hangs over both sides of the ideological spectrum. The Church will no longer persuade the masses to surrender to her teaching by fear of eternal damnation because capitalism with its transient materialism has dulled the need for transcendence and whatever it might imply. Poles have always had issues with authority given the history of the country, and, after the fall of communism, the authoritarian Church has become the new target of the groups seeking to discharge their existential malaise. As long as the Polish Pope John Paul II lived, the protests were moderate to respect his contribution to the fall of the Iron Curtain. Since his death in 2005, the standoff has intensified, dividing the country ideologically in a similar way to the divisions in the United States.

The questions that impose themselves to an uprooted individual in quest of identity who I have become is why so much strife, why so many quarrels, and, ultimately, why have we ended up having this war? The answer might be that the world has lost the sense of its true spiritual purpose. Instead of contemplating the order of the world and appreciating its existential beauty, humanity, in its rebellious impulse, has relinquished its organic dependency on the rest of the natural world order and opted for fashioning ideologies meant to free it from the existential gravity that linked it to nature. It has built these ideologies on the appeal to force thinking that it will free itself from religion, biology, and the laws of physics. In the process of conceiving this artificial paradise, it has plunged into oppression, despotism, and wars of conquest.

In this paradoxical endeavor of improving human condition here below on Earth, humanity uprooted itself; it severed its organic connection to the world order as it is. Marxism, derivative of Christianity, aborted the sphere of the divine for the benefit of the unrestricted use of force in its prophetic concept of the world. Concentration camps, labor camps, famines, massive executions, all were justified in the name of the providential progress warranted by the laws of history. Capitalism reconquered those territories promising a return to the natural laws of economy, showing that material enrichment is all good and inscribed in the providential design accepted by the God who likes the rich winners more than the poor losers. This is our world suspended between diverse ideologies aiming to divert from the essence of the human predicament: *malheur.*

Having tasted the hunger for material goods in the Poland of my youth, having entered the Western world with its material opulence but entangled in deceitful ideologies, having returned to free Poland to see that freedom could be a burden, I felt utterly uprooted with no hope for finding any grounding in the political world as we know it. Encounters with a few thinkers who directed my attention to the thought of Simone Weil and Leszek Kołakowski, later to Tzvetan Todorov's, I began to realize that my innate pessimistic outlook on the world would still not go away even if I were to accept any of the contemporary cultures. One thing was clear to me: I firmly knew that I could not detach myself from my religious upbringing in Catholicism. Tasso, Corneille, and my professor of 17th-century French literature implicitly reconnected my doctoral work with my Parisian experience of a "pion" (discipline enforcer) in a Jesuit school. It was my introduction to the way of dealing with *malheur* in a constructive fashion.

The experience of graduate school at Berkeley, with its joys and frustrations, has led to a synthesis of my life experience. It has instigated a rebellious attitude against the path my adoptive country's culture was indicating to me. Uprooted as I felt, my faith ingredient was like that residual bamboo root severed from the taproot of the plant by the gardener tired of its presence in his backyard. It would not go away, it would not die out. In the dark night of the soul, it pierced the layers of ideological deposits that were hiding it from the light, true light. I reconnected with those encounters in my life that have never left me in my cosmopolitan adventures: my imperfect religious upbringing.

This book is in fact a spiritual exercise in the Jesuit tradition I have learned to practice once I integrated this religious order some 20 years ago. It invites one to review one's life periodically to try to recognize how the spirit might have operated in one's life. The French philosopher Pierre Hadot[3] has applied the notion of spiritual exercise to philosophical discourse in general. He proposes the following definition of it: "Personally, I would define the spiritual exercise as a voluntary, personal practice, intended to operate a transformation of the individual, a transformation of oneself" (145). The *Spiritual Exercises* of Ignatius of Loyola are the heirs of Antiquity transmitted by monks who had been first to use the term to denote their spiritual practices (152). When Plato says in *Phaedo*, according to Hadot, that to practice philosophy is to train in dying, he means to separate oneself from the body and from the viewpoint both sensuous and selfish that the body imposes (145).

[3.] See the chapter titled "The Philosophical Discourse as Spiritual Exercise," in Pierre Hadot, *Philosophy as a Way of Life* (Paris: Albin Michel, 2001, my translation), 145–158.

In writing this text, I have sought to look, in the twilight of my existence, for what has really mattered in my life. While putting the word "misfit" in the title, I did not intend to undermine the contribution of my American experience to my spiritual growth. This spiritual exercise has taught me in fact that my spiritual journey would not have been possible without glimpses of genuine earthly happiness I have had in this utopia achieved called America from which the Spirit has led me out toward the path to the utopia that will hopefully be achieved in a different realm.

BIBLIOGRAPHY

Alighieri, Dante. *Dante's Inferno*. Translated by Mark Musa. Bloomington: Indiana University Press, 1971

Arendt, Hannah. *The Origins of Totalitarianism*. New York: Harcourt Brace Jovanovich, 1973.

Baudrillard, Jean. *America*. Translated by Chris Turner. London; New York: Verso, 1988.

Bertolucci, Bernardo, director. *Prima della rivoluzione* [Before the Revolution]. Iride Cinematografica, 1964.

Byrnes, Timothy A. "The Catholic Church and Poland's Return to Europe." *East European Quarterly* 30 (1996): 433–148.

Cave, Terence. *The Cornucopian Text: Problems of Writing in the French Renaissance*. Oxford: Oxford University Press, 1979.

Corneille, Pierre. *Oeuvres complètes* [Complete Works], edited by André Stegmann. Paris: Editions du Seuil, 1963.

Finkielkraut, Alain. *La défaite de la pensée* [The Undoing of Thought]. Paris: Gallimard, 1987.

———. *L'humanité perdue* [Lost Humanity]. Paris: Editions du Seuil, 1996.

———. *A la première personne* [In the First Person]. Paris: Gallimard, 2019.

Fumaroli, Marc. *Héros et orateurs: rhétorique et dramaturgie cornélienne* [Heroes and Orators: Corneille's Rhetoric and Dramaturgy]. Genève: Droz, 1990.

Hadot, Pierre. "Le discours philosophique comme exercice spirituel" [Philosophical Discourse as Spiritual Exercise]. In *La Philosophie comme manière de vivre. Entretiens avec Jeannie Carlier et Arnold J. Davidson* [Philosophy as a Way of Life. Interviews with Jeannie Carlier and Arnold Davidson], 144–158. Albin Michel Biblio essais, le Livre de Poche. Paris: Albin Michel, 2001.

Harrigan, Patrick J. "Church, State, and Education in France from the Fallout to the Ferry Laws: A Reassessment." *Canadian Journal of History* 36, no. 1 (April 2001): 51–83.

Ignatius, of Loyola, Saint. *The Spiritual Exercises of St. Ignatius Loyola.* Translated by Elisabeth Meier Tetlow. Lanham, MD: University Press of America, 1987.

Isakowicz-Zaleski, Tadeusz. *Księża wobec bezpieki na przykładzie archidiecezji krakowskiej* [Polish Priests and the Communist Secret Police]. Kraków: Znak, 2007.

Kołakowski, Leszek. "PRL—Wesoły nieboszczyk?" [Polish People's Republic—A Merry Corpse?] (My translation). First published in *Tygodnik Powszechny*, 1995 (7); republished in *Niepewność epoki demokracji* [The Uncertainty of the Age of Democracy], 70–84, quote 78.

————. "What the Past Is For?" Speech delivered in the Coolidge Auditorium, Library of Congress, November 5, 2003, upon reception of the first Kluge Prize. https://www.loc.gov/loc/lcib/0312/kluge3.html.

————. *Main Currents of Marxism: The Founders, the Golden Age, the Breakdown.* Translated by P.S. Falla. New York: W.W. Norton & Company, 2005.

————. "Dziedzictwo leftyzmu" [Heritage of Leftism]. In *Niepewność epoki demokracji* [The Uncertainty of the Age of Democracy], 35–44. Kraków: Znak, 2013. First published in *Kultura*, Paris, 1996, 1–2.

————. "W imię braterstwa czy w imię zniszczenia" [For Brotherhood or for Destruction]. In *Niepewność epoki demokracji* [The Uncertainty of the Age of Democracy], 16–28. Kraków: Znak, 2014.

————. "PRL—Wesoły nieboszczyk?" [Polish People's Republic—A Merry Corpse?]. In *Niepewność epoki demokracji* [The Uncertainty of the Age of Democracy], 70–84. Kraków: Znak, 2014.

————. "Ta diabelska wolność. Rozmyślania o złu" [This Devil's Freedom. Meditations on Evil]. In *Niepewność epoki demokracji* [The Uncertainty of the Age of Democracy], 147–157. Kraków: Znak, 2014.

————. "Demokracja jest przeciwna naturze" [Democracy Is against Nature]. In *Niepewność epoki demokracji* [The Uncertainty of the Age of Democracy], 169–177. Kraków: Znak, 2014.

Kramsch, Claire. *The Multilingual Subject: What Foreign Language Learners Say About Their Experience and Why It Matters.* Oxford: Oxford University Press, 2009.

Lepak, Keith John. *Prelude to Solidarity: Poland and the Politics of the Gierek Regime.* Columbia University Press, 1989.

McCullough, Lissa. *The Religious Philosophy of Simone Weil.* London; New York: I.B. Tauris & Co Ltd., 2014.

Miłosz, Czesław. Forward to *My Century* by Aleksander Wat. Translated by Richard Lourie. New York: NYRB, 1980, xx–xxi.

Monticone, Roland C. "The Catholic Church in Poland, 1945–1966." *The Polish Review* 11, no. 4 (Autumn 1966): 75–100.

Orwell, George. *Nineteen Eighty-Four.* London: Secker & Warburg, 1949.

Ricoeur, Paul. *Temps et Récit* [Time and Narrative]. Paris: Editions du Seuil, 1983.

———. *Time and Narrative.* vol. 1. Translated by Kathleen McLaughlin and David Pellauer. Chicago: University of Chicago Press, 1986.

———. *From Text to Action: Essays in Hermeneutics,* II. Translated by Kathleen Blamey & John B. Thomson. Evanston: Northwestern University Press, 1991.

———. "Mimesis and Representation." In *A Ricoeur Reader: Reflection and Imagination,* edited by Mario J. Valdés, 137–155. Toronto: Toronto University Press, 1991.

———. "Narrated Time." In *A Ricoeur Reader: Reflection and Imagination.* Edited by Mario J. Valdés, 338–354. Toronto: Toronto University Press, 1991.

———. "Narrative Identity." Translated by David Wood. In *On Paul Ricoeur: Narrative and Interpretation,* edited by David Wood, 188–199. Warwick Studies in Philosophy and Literature. London: Routledge, 1991.

———. "Time Traversed: Remembrance of Things Past." In *A Ricoeur Reader: Reflection and Imagination,* edited by Mario J. Valdés, 355–89. Toronto: Toronto University Press, 1991.

————. *Philosophie, éthique et politique: Entretiens et dialogues* [Philosophie, Ethics, and Politics: Interviews and Dialogues]. Edited by Catherine Goldenstein. Paris: Editions du Seuil, 2017.

Rubin, Rebecca B., Carlos Fernández Collado, and Roberto Hernandez-Sampieri. "A Cross-Cultural Examination of Interpersonal Communication Motives in Mexico and the United States." *International Journal of Intercultural Relations* 16, no. 2 (March 1992): 145–157.

Tasso, Torquato. *Gerusalemme liberata* [Jerusalem delivered]. Edited by Bruno Maier. Milan: Biblioteca Universale Rizzoli, 1982.

Tischner, Józef. *Nieszczęsny dar wolności* [The Unfortunate Gift of Freedom]. Kraków: Znak, 1998 (my translation).

Todorov, Tzvetan. *L'homme dépaysé* [The Man Out of His Homeland]. Paris: Editions du Seuil, 1996.

————. *The Totalitarian Experience.* Translated by Teresa Lavender Fagan. Seagull Books. Chicago: University of Chicago Press, 2011.

Wajda, Andrzej, director. *Danton.* Gaumont, 1983.

Weil, Simone. *The Need for Roots.* Translated by Arthur Wills. London: Routledge & Kegan Paul, 1952.

————. *L'Iliade ou le poème de la force* [The Iliad or the Poem of Force]. Paris: Editions Payot & Rivages, 2014.

————. *Note sur la suppression générale des partis politiques* [Note on the general abolition of political parties]. Paris: L'Herne, 2014.

Zanussi, Krzysztof, director. *From a Far Country.* Trans World Film, 1981.

www.ingramcontent.com/pod-product-compliance
Lightning Source LLC
Chambersburg PA
CBHW051219150426
42812CB00053BA/2525